"This remarkable collection of case studies sheds light on one of the least understood and yet crucially important aspects of contemporary theater practice: the role of the dramaturg. By turns, innovator, instigator, cultural historian, interpreter, provocateur, and visionary, the dramaturg shapes the lived experience of actors and audiences alike. In an illuminating introduction and a moving epilogue, Philippa Kelly shows that the diverse and distinctive voices assembled here are agents of radical change in the theater and in the world beyond its boundaries."

– **Stephen Greenblatt**, author of *Will in the World: How Shakespeare Became Shakespeare*

"This exploration of the multi-faceted craft of dramaturgy challenges readers, educators and theatre makers to do more – much more – to make theatre genuinely, intentionally and seriously inclusive. Always grounded in the pragmatics of theatre practice, this collection is much needed, a treasure house of ideas, debates and daring, expertly curated and illuminatingly introduced by Philippa Kelly."

– **Elizabeth Schafer**, Professor of Drama, Dance, and Theatre at Royal Holloway, University of London

"Philippa Kelly has been doing pioneering work in dramaturgy for many years. In this collection of remarkably intimate essays she gathers a community of likeminded practitioners, each committed to enhancing the truth and urgency of contemporary theatre. For Kelly and her peers, the dramaturg does far more than serve playtext, director, and cast. The dramaturg sounds the pulse of the collective moment, what Hamlet calls its 'form and pressure'. The attention thereby entailed must always be scrupulously local, alert to each exchange's multifarious particulars; nothing is achieved, nothing is *changed,* by rehearsing generalities or by iterative obedience. Theatre is no more and no less than the weathervane of democracy, attuned to its weather like no other medium. Listen to these voices, and the future is in good hands."

– **Simon Palfrey**, Professor, Brasenose College, University of Oxford

T0347951

Diversity, Inclusion, and Representation in Contemporary Dramaturgy

Diversity, Inclusion, and Representation in Contemporary Dramaturgy offers fresh perspectives on how dramaturgs can support a production beyond rigid disciplinary expectations about what information and ideas are useful and how they should be shared.

The sixteen contributors to this volume offer personal windows into dramaturgy practice, encouraging theater practitioners, students, and general theater-lovers to imagine themselves as dramaturgs newly inspired by the encounters and enquiries that are the juice of contemporary theater. Each case study is written by a dramaturg whose body of work explores important issues of race, cultural equity, and culturally-specific practices within a wide range of conventions, venues, and communities. The contributors demonstrate the unique capacity of their craft to straddle the ravine between stage and stalls, intention and impact.

By unpacking, in the most up-to-date ways, the central question of "Why this play, at this time, for this audience?," this collection provides valuable insights and dramaturgy tools for scholars and students of Dramaturgy, Directing, and Theater Studies.

Philippa Kelly is Resident Dramaturg for the California Shakespeare Theater; Professor and Chair of English at the California Jazz Conservatory; Adjunct Professor at the University of California, Berkeley; and Visiting Senior Fellow at the University of New South Wales in Australia.

Focus on Dramaturgy
Series Editor: Magda Romanska

The *Focus on Dramaturgy* series from Routledge – developed in collaboration with TheTheatreTimes.com – is devoted to the craft of dramaturgy from multiple contemporary perspectives. This groundbreaking comprehensive series is authored by top professionals in the field, addressing a variety of current hot topics in dramaturgy.

The series is edited by Magda Romanska, an author of the critically-acclaimed *Routledge Companion to Dramaturgy*, dramaturg, writer, theatre scholar, and Editor-in-Chief of TheTheatreTimes.com.

Words for the Theatre
David Cole

Principles of Dramaturgy
Robert Scanlan

New Dramaturgies
Strategies and Exercises for 21st Century Playwriting
Mark Bly

Dramaturgy of Migration
Staging Multilingual Encounters in Contemporary Theatre
Edited by Yana Meerzon and Katharina Pewny

Diversity, Inclusion, and Representation in Contemporary Dramaturgy
Case Studies from the Field
Edited by Philippa Kelly

For more information about this series, please visit: https://www.routledge.com/performance/series/RFOD

Diversity, Inclusion, and Representation in Contemporary Dramaturgy

Case Studies from the Field

Edited by Philippa Kelly

Editorial Associate: Amrita Ramanan

Routledge
Taylor & Francis Group

LONDON AND NEW YORK

First published 2020
by Routledge
4 Park Square, Milton Park, Abingdon, Oxon OX14 4RN

and by Routledge
605 Third Avenue, New York, NY 10017

First issued in paperback 2022

Routledge is an imprint of the Taylor & Francis Group, an informa business

© 2020 selection and editorial matter, Philippa Kelly; individual chapters, the contributors

The right of Philippa Kelly and Amrita Ramanan to be identified as the authors of the editorial material, and of the authors for their individual chapters, has been asserted in accordance with sections 77 and 78 of the Copyright, Designs and Patents Act 1988.

Publisher's Note
The publisher has gone to great lengths to ensure the quality of this reprint but points out that some imperfections in the original copies may be apparent.

British Library Cataloguing-in-Publication Data
A catalogue record for this book is available from the British Library

Library of Congress Cataloging-in-Publication Data
A catalog record for this book has been requested

ISBN 13: 978-1-03-247463-2 (pbk)
ISBN 13: 978-1-138-33445-8 (hbk)
ISBN 13: 978-0-429-44531-6 (ebk)

DOI: 10.4324/9780429445316

Typeset in Times New Roman
by Apex CoVantage, LLC

Contents

About the contributors

Izumi Ashizawa (director/playwright/performer/puppet-mask and costume designer) is the artistic director of Izumi Ashizawa Performance and Associate Professor of Devising Theatre and Performance Art at State University of New York at Stony Brook. Originally founded in 2002, Izumi Ashizawa Performance explores physical storytelling with unconventional puppetry and object animation and masks. Based on Japanese physical performance techniques, Ashizawa's movement techniques are taught around the world, and her devised pieces have been performed internationally, including in the US, Japan, the U.K., Canada, Norway, Russia, Austria, Bulgaria, Slovenia, Romania, Poland, Turkey, Iran, Australia, the Cayman Islands, Peru, Cyprus, and Estonia. Ashizawa has won numerous awards, including the Medal of Honor for Cultural Excellence from the City of Piura in Peru, the Capital Fringe Director's Award, the UNESCO-Aschberg Award, and the Tehran Municipality Culture & Arts Award. She is a graduate of the Yale School of Drama. Recent works: "I Cried Because I Had No Shoes Until . . ." commissioned by Physical Fest, U.K., 2019; "Bacchae" commissioned by Ancient Greek Drama Festival, Cyprus, 2019. Upcoming works: *Nalunaajaasuaraq* at Greenland National Theatre, 2020. This show will tour to different Inuit communities in Greenland. Opera, *Madama Butterfly*, at Opera Saratoga, N.Y., 2020.

Mark Bly has, over the past 35 years, served as Dramaturg/Associate Artistic Director at many leading resident theaters and on Broadway, dramaturging and producing more than 250 plays. Broadway credits include Emily Mann's *Execution of Justice* (1985), Moises Kaufman's *33 Variations* (2009), and Henrik Ibsen's *Enemy of the People* (2012) with Doug Hughes. He has dramaturged the world premieres of plays by Rajiv Joseph, Suzan Lori-Parks, Moises Kaufman, Tim Blake Nelson, Sarah Ruhl, and Ken Lin. He was Director of the MFA Playwriting Program at the Yale School of Drama from 1992–2004. Mark has written regularly for Yale Theatre as Contributing Editor/Advisory Editor. He is Editor for the Theater Communications Group's series *Production Notebooks: Theatre in Process: Volumes I & II* (1996, 2001), a project that was the inspiration for this volume. His current book, *New Dramaturgies: Strategies and Exercises for 21st Century Playwriting*, was released with Routledge in August 2019. Mark received the LMDA G.E. Lessing Career Achievement Award in 2010, and in 2019 he was awarded the Kennedy Center Medallion of Excellence for his outstanding lifetime contribution to American theater. Mark is an Ambassador at Large and on the Literary Reading Committee for the National New Play Network. He founded the LMDA Bly Fellowship/Creative Capacity Grant Fund for Innovative Dramaturgy, which made this volume possible.

Faedra Chatard Carpenter is a professional dramaturg, theatrer and performance studies scholar, and cultural critic. An Associate Professor in the School of Theatre, Dance, and Performance Studies at the University of Maryland, College Park, Dr. Carpenter was honored with the 2019 American Theatre and Drama Society's Betty Jean Jones Award for Outstanding Teacher of American Theatre and Drama. Through her analysis of both staged performances and the performative practices of everyday life, Dr. Carpenter applies her expertise in expressive culture, creative collaboration, and dramaturgical methodologies to forge common understandings and illuminate issues regarding race, gender, class, and sexuality. As a professional dramaturg, she has worked on productions at venues such as Mosaic Theater Company, Baltimore Center Stage, the John F. Kennedy Center for the Performing Arts, Dance Place, Crossroads Theatre Company, and Arena Stage. She is the author of the award-winning book *Coloring Whiteness: Acts of Critique in Black Performance*, and her scholarly analyses can be also be found in a number of anthologies and peer-reviewed journals such as *Theatre Survey, Theatre Topics, Women & Performance, The Routledge Companion to Dramaturgy, The Cambridge Companion to African American Theatre, MLA's Approaches to Teaching the Plays of August Wilson, Theater,* and *The Journal of Dramatic Theory and Criticism.*

Michael M. Chemers holds an MFA in playwriting from Indiana University (1997) and a PhD in theatre history and theory from the University of Washington (2001). He is Professor of Dramatic Literature at the University of California Santa Cruz, where he has taught since 2012. Prior to that time, he was Professor of Dramatic Literature at Carnegie Mellon University's School of Drama, where he founded and directed the Bachelor of Fine Arts in Production Dramaturgy Program. Michael is the creator of the 'Ghost Light' model of dramaturgy. Through his writings, which have been translated into several languages, this model has become popular across the world.

Walter Byongsok Chon is Assistant Professor of Dramaturgy and Theatre Studies at Ithaca College. He has served as dramaturg at the Yale Repertory Theatre, Yale School of Drama, the Eugene O'Neill Theatre Center, the Great Plains Theater Conference, the Hangar Theatre, the Civic Ensemble, and the New York Musical Festival. His writings appeared in *Theater, Praxis, The Korean National Theatre Magazine, The Korean Theatre Review, Asymptote, The Mercurian, The Routledge Companion to Dramaturgy*, and the online magazine *The Theatre Times*, for which he is serving as a co-managing editor for South Korea. His theatrical translations include *Inching Towards Yeolha* (Korean to English), Charles Mee's *True Love* (English to Korean), and Dürrenmatt's *The Doppelganger* (German to English). Walter received his BA in English from Sungkyunkwan University in Korea, his MA in theatre studies from Washington University in St. Louis, and his MFA in dramaturgy and dramatic criticism from Yale School of Drama, where he is completing his doctoral dissertation on romantic irony.

Tim Collingwood is an actor, playwright, and stage manager in the Cleveland, Ohio, area. He is also politically active and is a member of the Committee of 500 Years of Dignity and Resistance and the Cleveland Democratic Socialists of America. He is a proud uncle of two nieces and two nephews. When not changing the world through art and activism, he enjoys classic cinema, cooking, and learning new languages. He recently had a workshop production of an ability-positive retelling of "The Ugly Duckling" at Talespinner Children's Theatre and is about to workshop a play with the tentative title *Tell the Brethren About the Roman Catholic Women Priesthood Movement* at Cleveland Public Theatre.

Annalisa Dias is a citizen artist, community organizer, and award-winning theater-maker working at the intersection of racial justice and care for the earth. She is Director of Artistic Partnerships and Innovation at Baltimore Center Stage. Annalisa is also a producing playwright with The Welders, a DC playwright's collective; co-founder of the DC Coalition for Theatre & Social Justice; and co-founder of Groundwater Arts. Selected writing credits include *4380 Nights, the earth that is sufficient, One Word More, The Last Allegiance, A Legacy of Chains*, and *Servant of the Wind*. Annalisa's plays have been produced or developed by The Welders, Theater Alliance, Signature Theatre (DC), the Phillips Collection, The Gulfshore

Playhouse, the Mead Theatre Lab, The Hub Theatre, Spooky Action Theater, Tron Theatre (Glasgow), and Theatre 503 (London). Annalisa frequently teaches Theater of the Oppressed and decolonization workshops nationally and internationally and speaks about race, identity, and performance.

Julie Felise Dubiner is a dramaturg, producer, and teacher. Most recently, she was Associate Director of *American Revolutions* at the Oregon Shakespeare Festival. She was previously Resident Dramaturg at Actors Theatre of Louisville and the Prince Music Theater and has freelanced with Steppenwolf, Defiant, blue Star, the O'Neill, and more. She is the co-author of *The Process of Dramaturgy*, the co-editor of several volumes of Humana Festival plays, and a contributor to *The Routledge Companion to Dramaturgy*, *Innovation in Five Acts*, *HowlRound*, and other publications and podcasts. Julie is also a mentor for the LMDA Early Career Dramaturg caucus.

Martine Kei Green-Rogers is Assistant Professor of Theatre Arts at SUNY: New Paltz, a freelance dramaturg, and president of the Literary Managers and Dramaturgs of the Americas. She obtained her BA in theatre from Virginia Wesleyan College (now Virginia Wesleyan University), her MA in theatre history and criticism from The Catholic University of America, and her PhD in theatre from the University of Wisconsin-Madison. Her dramaturgical credits include work with the Louisville Orchestra, Pioneer Theatre Company, Plan-B Theatre, the Classical Theatre Company, Court Theatre, the Goodman, CATCO, and the Oregon Shakespeare Festival. Her publications include articles in *The Routledge Companion to Dramaturgy* and *Theatre History Studies*. She is currently working on a manuscript entitled *In The Studio: Dramaturgy and Stage Design* with Jesse Portillo, with Southern Illinois University Press.

Scott Horstein's freelance dramaturgy credits include Denver Center, Oregon Shakespeare Festival, Berkeley Rep, San Diego Rep, and the Old Globe. Scott formerly served in staff dramaturgy positions at Cornerstone Theater Company and the Black Dahlia Theater in Los Angeles. He currently serves as Associate Professor of Contemporary Theatre and Dramaturgy at Sonoma State University, where he also helps lead the campus Arts Integration Program as SSU Arts Dramaturg.

Ajuawak Kapashesit's plays have been performed in Minneapolis and Los Angeles. In 2018, Kapashesit was chosen as an Indigenous Film Opportunity Fellow with the Sundance Film Institute. He was one of the inaugural recipients of the Jay Switzer Comweb/William F. White International Indigenous Creator Award.

Dr. Philippa Kelly is Resident Dramaturg for the California Shakespeare Theater. She has published 100 refereed and commissioned articles and eleven books with international presses including Palgrave Press, Oxford University Press, Michigan University Press, the University of Western Australia Press, Ashgate Press, and John Benjamins Press, the closest to her heart being *The King and I* (Arden Press, 2011, 2012). A meditation on Australian identity through the lens of Shakespeare's *King Lear*, *The King and I* seeks to illuminate contemporary social attitudes toward those who are forced onto the fringes of society. Besides the California Shakespeare Theater, Philippa's production dramaturgy credits include the Oregon Shakespeare Festival, the Aurora Theatre, the Berkeley Repertory Theater, Word for Word, Ubuntu Theater Collective, Bare Stage productions, the Play On initiative, and Royal Holloway. Philippa is the recipient of Fulbright, Rockefeller, Humanities Research Council, and Commonwealth fellowships at UC Berkeley, Oxford University, and Bellagio, as well as from several Australian universities, including the University of New South Wales, where she currently serves as Visiting Senior Fellow. She is the co-recipient of a Bly Award for Innovation in Dramaturgy from the Literary Managers and Dramaturgs of the Americas and has received awards from the Walter and Elise Haas Foundation (2016, 2017) and the California Arts Council (2018–19) for her creation and leadership of dramaturgy programs for underserved schools.

Finn Lefevre is a dramaturg, applied theater facilitator, and educator. Their work combines trans and queer theories with restorative and collective healing powers of physical theater. They have taught in the theater departments at the University of Massachusetts and Keene State College and the Ethnic and Gender Studies Department at Westfield State University. They facilitate workshops in Theater of the Oppressed and Cops in the Head (Augusto Boal), story circles, somatic movement, and trans and queer performance.

Awele (Ah-WAY-lay) Makeba, a teacher of theater at Skyline High School, Oakland, has performed around the world, including the Kennedy Center for the Performing Arts, The Musikverein Vienna, Tsinchu Teacher's College in Taiwan, Suriname (US Dept. of State Tour), Russia, Australia, France, and Canada. Awele is an award-winning and internationally known storyteller/teaching artist, literacy specialist, and recording artist recognized as a "truth teller" and an artist for social change. She researches, writes, and performs hidden African American history, folklore, and personal tales. She provides opportunities for audiences to grapple with the meaning of their own lives as they make meaning of past lives. She has made it her life's work to tell history through the words of its silenced and oft-forgotten witnesses. Awele teaches through performance, and she animates democracy through her art.

Jonathan Meth continues to work as Project Dramaturg with an expanded Crossing The Line Partnership (discussed in his chapter) on Ogmius, an EU Erasmus+ funded training project, and Trasna Na Line, an EU Creative Europe funded collaboration. This partnership will feature the next Crossing The Line Festival in Galway May 20–23, 2020, as part of the European Capital of Culture. He is curator of The Fence, an international network of 250 playwrights and theater-makers from fifty countries, which he set up in 2003. He is Associate Lecturer on the MA in Arts Administration & Cultural Policy at the Institute for Creative & Cultural Entrepreneurship, Goldsmiths, University of London and Visiting Fellow at the Department of Film, Theatre and Television at the University of Reading (2017–20).

Amrita Ramanan is Director of Literary Development and Dramaturgy at the Oregon Shakespeare Festival, where her production dramaturgy credits include *Henry IV* Parts 1 and 2, *Henry V*, *Oklahoma!*, *Snow in Midsummer*, *As You Like It*, *Cambodian Rock Band*, *Macbeth*, and *Alice in Wonderland*. She is the producer of OSF's Black Swan Lab for New Play Development. Previous to her tenure at OSF, Amrita was Associate Producer and Resident Dramaturg for Double Edge Theater in Ashfield, Massachusetts, and Artistic Associate and Literary Manager for Arena Stage in Washington, DC. She has received numerous accolades for her work in "living culture" for community engagement, collaborative exchange, and cross-sector partnerships that foster equity, diversity, and inclusion, and in 2016 she won a Bly Innovation Award (with Alison Carey) from the Literary Managers and Dramaturgs of the Americas for a project in Greenturgy. Amrita serves as board member for the Literary Managers and Dramaturgs of the Americas and the Network of Ensemble Theaters. She received a BFA in dramaturgy and theater history from the University of Arizona.

Mei Ann Teo is a theater- and film-maker who works at the intersection of artistic/civic/contemplative practice. As a director/devisor/dramaturg, she collaborates internationally across genres, including multi-form performance and music theater. Her main collaborators include the multi-hyphenates Diana Oh, Jillian Walker, Nia Witherspoon, and Raquel Almazan. Mei Ann was the director featured at the MIT's Symposium Next Wave: The Future of Asian American Theatre and has presented at national conferences including the Literary Managers and Dramaturgs of the Americas, Association for Theatre in Higher Education, Consortium of Asian American Theaters and Artists, Network of Ensemble Theatres, and Arts In the One World. She was Professor of Directing and Dramaturgy at Hampshire College and Chair of Drama at Pacific Union College. She is Producing Artistic Director of Musical Theatre Factory, a Resident Company of Playwrights Horizons.

Preface

How do responses to race, ethnicity, gender, religion, sexual orientation, disability, and other social locations impact the way theater is made and received? What kinds of biases block an artist's capacity to explore and address aspects of identity? The very word "diverse" derives from "two" (i.e. "more than one") ways of following a verse or direction. This is the juice of theater – to see, hear, and interpret in multi-vocal and challenging ways. Key to theater-making is the role of the dramaturg, who generates the connective tissue between many areas of a production process. A dramaturg explores context, works intimately with directors, helps calibrate the way a script is opened out in rehearsal, and provides conduits for audience reception and conversation.

Dramaturgs share with all theater artists the endeavor to engage with society, with history, with perspectives of otherness and outsiderness. In making *Diversity, Inclusion, and Representation in Contemporary Dramaturgy: Case Studies from the Field*, Amrita and I have drawn together contributors whose case studies attest to the fascination, power, and complexity of theater-making.

None of us has all the answers. We learn from each other.

Philippa Kelly
August 2019

Acknowledgments

We are honored to have commissioned this book with the invitation and support of Routledge *Focus on Dramaturgy* Series Editor Magda Romanska, funded by an inaugural Bly Award for Innovation in Dramaturgy from the Literary Managers and Dramaturgs of the Americas. Mark Bly, Brian Quirt, Cindy SoRelle, Martine Kei Green-Rogers, and the Literary Managers and Dramaturgs of the Americas (LMDA) have been a source of enduring and inspirational support. Special thanks to Sylvia Abrams, Emily Stone and Kate Van Riper, who stepped in at the end to give expert assistance with proofreading, and to Michael Chemers, who contributed patient and excellent reviews. Thanks also to designer Annie Smart, composer Paul Dresher, philosophers Chandran Kukathas and Martin Krygier, and (philosophically driven) Sharyn Charnas for their invaluable comments.

We are thrilled beyond words to have commissioned a series of chapters that emerge from the rich soil of theater-making to express and explore the possibilities opened up by dramaturgical creativity. And from the editor's perspective, through every single collaboration, I have learned far more than I have contributed.

Philippa Kelly and Amrita Ramanan
April 2020

Introduction

Dramaturgy in motion

Philippa Kelly

In 2018, as I prepared to apply for citizenship of the United States, I studied the Declaration of Independence as ratified in 1776. I read

> that all men are created equal, . . . endowed by their Creator with cer-
> tain unalienable rights, [and] that among these are Life, Liberty and the
> pursuit of Happiness.[1]

Since this document was adopted by the Continental Congress – a group of propertied white protestant men in Philadelphia – there has been a continual drive to expand the definition of who should be entitled to enjoy the blessings enumerated above. The Emancipation Proclamation of 1863 and the 13th Amendment of 1865; the 14th Amendment of 1868 that provided the right to vote and equal protection under the law for all males; the 15th Amendment in 1870, preventing states from denying any man the right to vote on grounds of "race, color, or previous condition of servitude"; the granting of women's suffrage in 1920 . . . these stand as some of the defining moments in American history. The Civil Rights Movement of the 1960s and the Voting Rights Act of 1965 – together with certain key Supreme Court decisions like *Brown v. Board of Education* (1954, racial segregation), *Roe v. Wade* (1973, abortion rights), and *Obergefell v. Hodges* (2015, same-sex marriage) – have shown "we the people" to be a protean, multi-headed creature that can struggle, and prove itself by law, to be true democracy in action.

While Martin Luther King gave faith to millions that the arc of the moral universe is long, eventually bending toward justice, it doesn't bend on its own. Moreover, we have arrived at a point where it is clear that laws alone cannot make it bend. Issues of inclusion, equity, and representation, involving deeply embedded conflicts and biases, continue to play out in the American political, cultural, and legal arenas to this day. Theater provides a vital expression of these critical issues in its capacity to portray, individual-to-individual, actions and consequences that are framed by larger social struggles.

The case studies in this volume detail some experiences with which dramaturgically-driven artists currently grapple in making theater. As dramaturgs we are conduits, sometimes lightning rods, for controversies that "play out" in theater spaces, including the connections (and the disconnects) that occur between stage and stalls. The work that we do is difficult to quantify or prescribe, but dramaturgy is fundamental to the creation of a concentrated theatrical "world" on stage: one that encourages audiences to explore motivations and to make critical investments while contemplating multiple perspectives. Theater can provoke emotional contagion and inspiration, inviting us to live in another person's body or worldview for a moment or a lifetime.

And why am I, Philippa, involved in this particular project? I am a white woman, an immigrant first from England and then from Australia. I grew up in a time when, through the "White Australia Policy," Australia opened its doors to white British people in order to color the country with the ideals of its colonial founders: the addition of every "Brit" consolidated the erasure of those who had inhabited "the Antipodes" for 40,000 years. This was how my family came to relocate in Australia – for 60 pounds total ($134.40 US, or just over $1,000 in today's currency), all seven of us were invited to fly to Australia – ironically, less than two centuries after my mother's ancestors on both sides were deported from England to Australia as criminals. The White Australia Policy remained in practice all through my early childhood and was abolished only in 1974.

From the age of fourteen when I was introduced to *King Lear* at my rural public high school, theater has been a vehicle through which I've contemplated the complexity of my family, the world, and the often paternalistic operations of authority. Australia's free undergraduate education, and thereafter a series of scholarships, afforded me many years of study in the field of theater and Shakespeare (with a special interest in *King Lear*). Theater has imbued my life with value and helped me to make meaning. And as an active member of a theater community in the United States today, I have in recent years been increasingly intrigued and challenged by the lenses of diversity, representation, and inclusion.

I recall my young self at a local Australian country store. The store manager reached over the people in front of me – indigenous Australians – and said, "Can I help you, Miss?" There was a queue that was invisible to her. She saw only one white person. This moment remains illustrative of barriers – reaching way beyond the law and exercising their own cunning potency – that are non-existent to some, while being impassable for other's. I believe it is essential to question dynamics and interactions that arise from diverse racial backgrounds, from non-conforming gender identities, from disability labelling, from any process or perspective that relegates people to the periphery of social attention and value. My aim, as a practicing dramaturg and a writer, is to stretch the seams of how our profession has conventionally been defined: dramaturgy can be a vein that freshly animates information that may at first seem inert or benign: what is on a driver's license (age, gender); how bodies act in space, interacting with other bodies and objects; how a criminal record can affect one's relationship to; "citizenry" how individuals and institutions rank and delimit human and other life forms. Dramaturgical questions can prompt us to give new life and shape to other's expectations and our own.

Can a woman lead a Fortune 500 company? Of course she can. Can a man with authority be dismissed because he has abused people in his power? Of course he can. Can a person stand up and say, "This is not acceptable" and not be dismissed from employment for conveniently invented reasons? This question is more subtle and insidious, and I have had some experience of it in my own life. I once endured sustained gendered workplace harassment and sexual harassment in the midst of an apparently flourishing early career. Eventually I made a formal complaint. Powers that I didn't know existed rained down on my head, and I was served with papers to say that my contribution to my workplace – despite numerous awards and grants – would soon be terminated. I decided to fight this, and for a long period faced the social death that threatens people who reveal uncomfortable actualities and are met with denial, opposition, rejection, and ostracism. My situation was eventually resolved in a victory of sorts that I tucked away. It became a form of internal rupture that I strove to conceal from others and from myself. Almost two decades later this experience still has the power to grip me with self-doubt, rearing its head as if it happened only yesterday. But its reverberative power has also granted me my own perceptual entryway to aspects of the shaming, the anger, the reliance on institutions that fail us, the continued will to live and flourish, that is a part of the struggle of diversity and inclusion. The experience of being misrepresented, or not represented at all.

The assertion of individual identity is a way of saying, "I am here, I matter as a human being, I have a voice, and I won't shut up."

In the remainder of this contribution, I will introduce you to the chapters in *Diversity, Inclusion, and Representation in Contemporary Dramaturgy: Case Studies from the Field*, through my engagement with them as editor. The work of diversity, inclusion, and representation will always illuminate beautiful difference – "beautiful" because it is felt, examined, uniquely interpreted, though often born out of discomfort and pain – as readers bring their personal histories to how we receive and respond. Each of the case studies is exemplary in the sense that it reveals aspects of a wider social awareness or activism that dramaturgs have identified or been confronted with.

Welcome to this collection. This conversation.

1. Permission to speak

When funding productions and investing in theater companies, board members engage in a kind of dance, freighted by power on both sides – the power of artistic creativity on one side, the power of money and support on the other. Some board members realize this, taking up the dance with care, even with elegance, but others might unwittingly dance out of step and cause blisters. In our first case study, "Deconstructing Our Perspectives on Casting," Faedra Chatard Carpenter describes the power dynamics of a relationship she encountered in 2015. African American director Hana S. Sharif was invited to helm Christopher Baker's adaptation of *Pride and Prejudice* for Baltimore Center Stage, with Faedra as dramaturg. The two were approached by a white male patron who suggested that they should be offering opportunities to black actors. Only unenlightened white directors, he implied, would cast *Pride and Prejudice* in a nineteenth-century English world: artists of color would surely shake up that dynamic. But beneath the apparent compliment was the message: *Stage what you know. Authentic Austen is not your history.* The color of a director's skin should not determine the ways in which space, time, and values are bridged in finding a story's world centuries and continents apart; and donors who wield "donation-with-expectation" can make of the donor/artist dance an awkward and sometimes hurtful impediment to freedom of artistic movement.

In "Dramaturgy as Prophecy," Scott Horstein describes his own engagement with the question of who gets to speak and on what terms. In 2015 he staged *Facing Our Truth: Ten-Minute Plays on Trayvon, Race, and Privilege* at the Sonoma State student campus, comprised of six works written by eight playwrights, each of them ignited by the shooting of Trayvon Martin in 2012 and the subsequent exoneration of the killer, George Zimmerman, by a mostly white, all-female jury. Scott begins with an analysis of his own role as white male director/dramaturg who reflects on the artistic authority invested in the roles of director and dramaturg and the cultural and political authority involved in the process of casting – a process that is complicated by the often tiny casting pools available to a student production. Such difficulties and limitations often provoke artists to back away from projects that threaten a reactive political minefield in the face of artistic aspiration. To seek authentic community with those represented on stage, Scott suggests, is risky for a director/dramaturg's entitlement to integrity and self-worth. With all of this in mind, Scott felt compelled to stage the production. The voice of the courts has judged Zimmerman innocent, which makes it all the more important to stage the voices of grief, loss, fury, and confusion that make Trayvon's death such a potent moment in recent history.

Classrooms in underfunded schools are places where some inspired and resilient teachers are encouraging "permission to speak out." In "The Dramaturgy of the Classroom," teacher/artist/activist Awele Makeba opens a window into Skyline High School, famous for "producing" Tom Hanks in the 1970s and now an underserved school where theater is given the lowest priority in the budget and in class scheduling. I have been working as a resident artist with Awele, paying attention to her remarkable capacity to make theater a place of witnessing truth and of weaving old stories into new lives and frameworks. A book on diversity, equity, inclusion, and representation is enriched by a contribution from this inspirational teacher, through whose mentorship students learn the resourcefulness crucial to developing theater skills.

2. Taking up positions – playwright/dramaturg

In recent decades, perhaps the greatest worldwide transformation, besides climate change, is in our relationship to the internet. For a large proportion of the world, virtual communication has exploded into all areas of life. People are increasingly able or compelled to work from remote locations and to choose their hours of labor using a twenty-four-hour clock. But increased availability does not necessarily mean increased awareness or attention. We are easily persuaded to ignore information that we don't want to see (or that governments don't want us to see). Despite the ubiquity of the internet, the more disenfranchised peoples of the world still continue to suffer largely out of sight. This, I believe, makes theater even more urgent and valuable: it's a collective experience that we agree to engage in, using someone else's timing and someone else's space and witnessing someone else's ideas of what the world may look like.

Dramaturgs have a crucial role in what is represented on stage and how. In "The Dramaturgy of Black Culture," Martine Kai Green-Rogers addresses the need and capacity to interrupt conventional expectations. Together with director Robert OJ Parson, Martine has worked to complicate the dark paths of anger and despair that have often been flagged as trajectories for representing black identity in August Wilson's plays. By using dance and music, dramaturg and director have collaborated to shift the audience's ideas of how to approach Wilson's oeuvre, so that a "body of work" breaks apart into unique kinesthetic experiences.

In many of the chapters in this volume, indeed, I see dramaturgically driven artists breaking through – or away from – conventional practices in search of new and more innovative forms of representation. Izumi Ashizawa's case study (with Ajuawak Kapashesit), "Embodied Dramaturgy," prioritizes physicality. The "embodied" dramaturgy they share displaces conventional images of a dramaturg sitting at the back of a rehearsal room behind a pile of reference books. Izumi gives director Ajuawak Kapashesit a direct personal voice in her writing, representing – in the very "flesh" of her chapter – "embodied" dramaturgy's symbiotic presence in the rehearsal process. In focusing on movement in this way, Izumi's dramaturgy questions the binaries of dramaturg/scholar and director/activator. Through Izumi's practice as developed with Ajuawak, dramaturg and director move in physical and psychological tandem as they bring the staged work into being.

When I first read Finn Lefevre's case study, "The Name (Isn't a) Game," the words of the Old Testament rang through to me from countless childhood recitals of Isaiah 9:6: "For unto us a child is born . . . and he shall be called . . ." Finn's chapter begins with a call to re-evaluate the closure implicit in given names. Impact workshops are unsatisfying to Finn because they require participants to leave their names, together with all that they embody or signify, at the door. Why would Finn want to plane their identity down further when they have been socially compelled to enact a simplified version of their gendered identity every day? "In the Fall of 2016," Finn responded:

> Names can cause dysphoria, trigger memories of misgendering and being "clocked." They can build pride, as we choose our own new names or rebuild a relationship with a given name. Names can be a space of absence, when a new name lacks the history or familial connection usually a part of cisgender name narratives. But names can also be revolutionary, as gendered associations with names are stripped away, and our societal reliance on names is unpacked and dissolved. Thus was born the Trans Naming Workshop (TNW).
>
> (see this volume, p. 59)

The activities Finn describes encourage participants to re-examine their relationships with given names and to consider the impact of chosen names – transforming names from receptacles of received identity to powerful re-creations, newly connecting with chosen selves in intentional and compelling ways.

In "Translation and Form," Julie Felise Dubiner asks questions about the "relatability" and "clarity" that directors conventionally task dramaturgs with tracking. She begins her contribution with the premise:

> I'd like us to think about accepting plays in their own place. Their own language. And their own structure. Too often we ask the creators to translate them, or we judge them for steadfastly remaining in their own language.
>
> (see this volume, p. 63)

Julie means more than, for example, listening to a play in German – she means receiving a play in its own words, images, and unique forms of communication. She is tired of hearing the response to a play in rehearsal, "I feel like it's not done," which is often a signal that the piece doesn't satisfy conventional aesthetic and marketable norms. She advocates for theater makers to address our own forms of reception and communication, widening our range of responses, instead of seeing a play in terms of "lack" or "incompleteness." She asks us to reconsider dramaturgical questions like, "should the storytelling be clear?" The word "clear" can indeed serve as its own aesthetic straitjacket.

3. Who's "at the table?"

This section of this volume asks readers to think about who we expect to be taking big decisions in theater-making, a question that involves challenges to aesthetic premises and conventional power relationships. In "Crossing The Line," Jonathan Meth describes an ambitious international project he constructed, featuring learning-disabled artists from three companies in three different countries (see this volume, p. 75). Jonathan's approach to dramaturgy in learning-disabled contexts is that conversations about quality are about redistribution of power, and that "the hierarchies of theater reviewing need to be laid bare," allowing theater to be more truly diverse in its representation and reach. Sometimes connecting with a learning-disabled artist's world (for instance, someone with autism) may be like encountering someone from another country, with disorienting frames and lenses. Therefore, in conceiving Crossing The Line, Meth thought: why not *have* people from different countries, beginning with multiple languages as a way of deprioritizing language and straightforwardly representational communication? Crossing The Line began with a congress in which the first day, for each artist, was spent as audience to an unfamiliar tongue, kicking off a project that encouraged participants to find new expressive languages for theater-building. For Jonathan as dramaturg, this meant a focus on the connective possibilities of disruptive practices, which provoke artists to see and hear and feel in quite different ways.

In "*Depth Perception*," Tim Collingwood offers an analysis of a play he wrote to stage his own cognitive difference. Diagnosed early in life with Asperger's, Tim has been taught throughout his years to internalize disability by constantly practicing the cues of "normalcy." In writing and staging his own play about autism, he wanted to turn things around so that the normative world became audience to his world, taking autism out of the "disability" corridor and into a wider field that could be theatricalized, asking audiences to see, hear, and receive his "Aspie" self not as a condition but as a unique relationship to the world. Tim is honest and self-critical in his chapter, interrogating the audience's expectations as well as his own: how did his play measure up to ideas of a "successful" production? And what are the stakes in prioritizing actors with autism, as Tim did?

The notion of "familiar practice" is profoundly questioned also by Annalisa Dias, who, in "Decolonizing 'Equity, Diversity, and Inclusion,'" advocates the break-up of terms that repeat conservative modes of exclusion within supposedly inclusive frameworks (see this volume, p. 90). "Diversity," she argues, "is sought after for the purpose of increasing the economic value of institutions, which are still primarily owned and operated by white individuals." Invitations to sit at the table, lauded capacities to "check more than one box," the homogenization of native peoples as an extra racial category indicating self-congratulatory institutional "inclusion": all of this repeats a kind of cataloging that does not always genuinely or generously include, seeking instead to keep hold of the financial infrastructure of grant-making via self-marketing displays of inclusiveness. "The table" (and, indeed, "the room") are familiar structures by which white supremacy still recognizes its own primacy and seeks to bracket or contain and control otherness.

A self-consciously disruptive possibility for occupying theater space is offered in Mei Ann Teo's case study about her work on Diana Oh's *Lingerie* play, "Dramaturging Revolution." Mei Ann describes Diana Oh: "Diana Oh (she/they pronouns) is a queer Korean American performance artist/writer/ actor/singer-songwriter/theatermaker/artist of color multi-hyphenate." Mei Ann sees Diana Oh's performance space as one

> where agency and do-no-harm exist in sweet balance, [yet her piece] also holds furious anger. . . . It feels like a wide-open field of poppies for frolicking while unabashedly fighting our innermost shame demons.
> (see this volume, p. 102)

Such a performance gives artists and audiences a way to play *and* to do battle with corrosive underscores of social shaming and exclusion that still prevail in far too many unexamined places.

4. Cultural landscapes, past, present, and future

In recent years we have come to recognize that ideally every part of the theater-making process lives and breathes dramaturgy; dramaturgy doesn't "belong" to any one specific artist and is not contained and notated within one production notebook. This recognition informs Walter Byong-sok Chon's case study on Gao Xingjian's *The Other Shore*, "The Stakes of Expanding a Cultural Landscape," in which he considers how a play's reception and interpretation change in view of historical context. Walter's chapter has three different cultural points of entry: his addressing of geographical and historical background (*The Other Shore*'s precursor, *Bus Stop*, had been unaccountably associated with Theater of the Absurd and banned from China); issues of pre-assigned value, since the playwright had already received a Nobel Prize; and questions about how Chinese material would be understood in a very different culture. In considering these questions, Walter details how he approached the dramaturgy of this piece with the desire to enrich the audience's experience. For example, he included excerpts from Xingjian's Nobel Laureate lecture in his dramaturgical notes so that Gao Xingjian's political impact was deeply ingrained in the art-making process. Walter himself also took on an acting role, thus calibrating the two artistic contributions of dramaturg/performer. He notes that one of the beauties of the production was that the performers came from a heterogeneous group of countries, mirroring in their composition the very heterogeneity in Xingjian's play.

2017 saw a University of California Santa Cruz production of *Zoot Suit* directed by Kinan Valdez, forty years after his father Luis had written and staged the original work. In "Visit to a Zoot Planet," dramaturg Michael M. Chemers notes that the pachuco culture in Los Angeles originated among Mexican descendants living in El Paso, Texas, in which the zoot suit, with its long finger-tip jacket, wide lapels, high-waisted, full-cut trousers, elaborate vests, wide-collared shirt, and wide-brimmed hat was a symbol of cultural transgression. In the zoot suit, Latinos "wore" their restless and bold desire to establish an American identity that could disrupt and challenge the American Dream, resisting the white hegemony at the core of longed-for social prosperity and peace. Michael observes:

> Pachuquismo complicates a notion of America as a homogenous society, with a single language and culture, and exposes that notion as fundamentally racist and exclusionary.
>
> (see this volume, p. 123)

And so it does today, forty years on. In the context of *Zoot Suit*, Michael analyses the impact of the 2016 US presidential election on American culture: "an election that underscored the need for affirmative representations of American multiculturalism in brand-new ways." History, repeated, re-imagined, through the lens of theater.

On February 14, 1990, from a distance of more than four billion miles, the spacecraft *Voyager* photographed the universe in which the earth appeared as a mere point of light, a "pale blue dot." For astrophysicist Carl Sagan, that image is a reminder of something that Shakespeare also described in another context (*The Tempest*)[2] more than four centuries ago – the phenomenon of light that seems, to the viewer, magical. "The earth," says Sagan,[3]

> is a very small stage in a vast cosmic arena. Think of the rivers of blood spilled by all those generals and emperors so that in glory and triumph they can become the momentary masters of the fraction of a dot. . . . Our posturings, our imagined self-importance, the delusion that we have some privileged place in the universe, are challenged by this point of pale light.

For dramaturg Mark Bly, Sagan's metaphysical speculation highlights a series of moments that reach beyond the archives and into the living essence of what it means to be human. As inhabitants of the universe, we owe a debt and an obligation to all living creatures past, present, and future. Mark asks in his chapter, "The Dramaturgical Impulse – Or How Big is Your Universe?," Mark asks dramaturgs to think bigger, to aim, in the context and materials we provide, not for closure but for questions; imagining ourselves as part of a universal heartbeat that embraces the unknown.

And finally, there is my closing chapter, written on the wings of every contributor with whom I've had the great privilege to collaborate.

***

The case studies described here examine moments in dramaturgical practice that pose questions, presenting opportunities for dramaturgs to re-frame ideas and situations that can become crucial junctures for learning and growth. Questions that linger, and the difficulty of finding fully restorative answers, speak to the power of such moments. As theater artists, should we be surprised to find ourselves facing complexities and difficulties in addressing deeply-rooted social inequities as they play out, overtly or latently, in theater practice? No – we should expect them, be prepared to acknowledge them, and, to the best of our ability, use them to break new ground. If artists are going to make mistakes (and let's face it: we have and we will), we should at least try to make new mistakes rather than repeating the behaviors and myopias of the past.

A note on the text

- Readers will notice that in some chapters contributors refer to Black artists in the upper case, and in others they refer to "black" and "white." As editor I struggled with this for quite some time, wanting to follow publishing rules for normalization, yet feeling that such referencing is deeply personal. I have ended up deciding that contributors should feel able to choose their own form of referencing, and I ask for readers' acceptance of the level of variation.

- In my introductory chapter, I have chosen to refer to the authors by their first names. Our contributors themselves generally adhere to the convention of using last names, and again I ask for our readers' acceptance of contributors' preferences.

Notes

1 From the US Declaration of Independence, adopted by the Second Continental Congress meeting at the Pennsylvania State House in Philadelphia, Pennsylvania, on July 4, 1776.

2 In *The Tempest*'s second scene, Ariel describes to Prospero (referring to the phenomenon we now call St. Elmo's Fire, a little round light that trembles and streams in the wake of a storm):

> I boarded the king's ship, now on the beak,
> Now in the waist, the deck, in every cabin
> I flam'd amazement: sometimes I'd divide,
> And burn in many places: on the topmast,
> The yards and bowsprit, would I flame distinctly,
> Then meet and join.
>
> (Shakespeare, *The Tempest*, The Norton Shakespeare,
> edited by Stephen Greenblatt, et al. New York:
> W. W. Norton, 2000, I.ii, 194–200)

3 "Reflections on a Mote of Dust." http://www2.hawaii.edu/~davink/quoting.pdf

Section One

Permission to speak

1 Deconstructing our perspectives on casting

An "inter-article" with Hana S. Sharif

Faedra Chatard Carpenter

Reframing casting

In the world of theater, many are quick to think of casting in terms of the procedures and politics framing the assignment of performing artists – actors, singers, and/or dancers – to specific roles. Subsequently, the recognition of embodied or expressed differences, particularly as they may relate to what is visible to spectators (that is, corporeal markers of race, gender, age, size, ability, etc.) is always in consideration, both implicitly and explicitly. Whether or not casting choices are made with conscientious determination or with willful ignorance of their possible interpretive consequences, producing artists can never fully control the reception of their intentions: rather, they can only hope to avoid potential misinterpretations.[1]

While one may not think of casting as a multifarious concept in theater, it is. The matter of casting is not limited to what bodies we see when the proverbial curtain rises. It also pertains to a production's unseen yet undeniable impresarios – most notably, designers and directors. With the exception of those who self-appoint (for example, an artistic director who has the means to determine the directing assignments they will or will not take on), artistic leadership is also "cast." These appointments offer the same possibilities and pitfalls as when designating performers to particular roles or characters.

Whether one is selected as a consultant, dramaturg, designer, choreographer, or director, individuals have been "cast" in given roles as executors of artistic intentions. Consequently, their casting is aimed toward yet another form of casting: these chosen artists are charged with shaping what we see, hear, and feel. They are tasked to fit and fill a creative vision. These various renditions of casting always involve maneuvers of inclusion and exclusion. Casting can be understood as an act of luring, baiting. It is a method used to attract, compel, and catch particular impulses or interpretations. And just as there is the state of being "cast in," there is also the dynamic of being "cast out" – precluded, dismissed, and even freed.

Like a status indicator on Facebook, casting can be complicated.

Beginning with this comprehensive understanding of casting – and grounded in my firm belief that casting is always a dramaturgical consideration – this interview/article (or "inter-article") invites readers to contemplate how artistic leadership is often cast and how deviations from all-too-typical practices challenge both audiences and production stakeholders to confront narrow ways of thinking and doing. By fully recognizing the role of casting when it comes to artistic leadership, I hope to highlight how diversions from traditional expectations must be considered and championed in order to bring forth greater equity and manifest inclusive opportunities. In so doing, I lean on a conversation I recently had with a theater artist that I have known for quite a while and for whom I hold a great deal of admiration: Hana S. Sharif.

Hana S. Sharif made history in July 2018 when she was named the Artistic Director of the Repertory Theatre of St. Louis, becoming the first African American woman to lead a major League of Resident Theaters (LORT) playhouse. Acknowledging Sharif's groundbreaking appointment, this inter-article is propelled by the hope that Sharif will not simply be known as one of a very few stellar anomalies in the annals of American theater history; rather, it is my hope that Sharif's appointment will help serve as a catalyst that opens the gate for other female, African American artistic directors.[2] Serving as a generative example of "non-traditional casting" within the frame of artistic leadership, Sharif's experiences disclose the casting politics that still encumber our institutions, as well as the promising possibilities that abound when we are willing to deconstruct old perspectives about who is prepared to lead us into the future of American theater.

Confronting *Pride and Prejudice* with Hana Sharif

In 2015, I served as the dramaturg for *Pride and Prejudice* by Christopher Baker, a world premier adaptation directed by Baltimore Center Stage's (then) Associate Artistic Director, Hana S. Sharif (Figure 1.1). In our first dramaturgical meeting, Sharif emphasized two things: her great passion for the works of Jane Austen (she is able to speak on all six novels with vigor and insight) and her creative vision for this particular production. In discussing her vision for the play, Sharif highlighted the ways in which Austen artfully protested against the commodification of women's bodies and consistently created female characters that defy expectations. With specific reference to *Pride and Prejudice*, Sharif repeatedly expressed how Austen's novel prompts us to contemplate the role of social status in crafting our

Figure 1.1 Hana S. Sharif, Director of *Pride and Prejudice*, Baltimore Center Stage, 2015

Source: Photography credit Bill Geenen

belief-systems. Accordingly, the premise of "deconstructing perspectives" shaped how she saw the impulses and architecture of the characters' lives.

Carrying the premise and motif of "deconstructing perspectives" to the staging and design of Baltimore Center Stage's *Pride and Prejudice*,

Sharif directed the creation of a set that animated multiple "ways of see-ing." This was done through the use of picture frames and scenic windows that transformed to expose alternative scenes and simultaneous happenings, as well as through the employment of canvas panels that were either lit in order to become transparent enough to reveal moments "behind closed doors" or made opaque so as to host projections and filmed vignettes. The design inspired by Sharif's vision incorporated both live bodies and medi-ated images of various characters and, through its use of shadows and sil-houettes, conjured the art of the controversial (yet ever-fascinating) Kara Walker. This montage of imagery propelled the design to break through expectations of realism and invite a strategic clashing of perspectives. With its mix of genres, locations, and temporalities, the design activated Sharif's intent to retell a well-known story – full of familiar characters – in a fresh and unexpected way.

Without a doubt, Sharif's creative vision for *Pride and Prejudice* informed the design palettes of the production, impacting elements related to set, cos-tume, music, movement, lighting, and projection. Yet Baker's adapted text still paid due homage to the original novel, and, with deliberate conscious-ness, the actors were cast with an intentional adherence to the world as Austen envisioned it. In other words, the actors were all white folk. What proved to be surprising to some, however, was the fact that the all-white cast of *Pride and Prejudice* was being led by a Black woman and, moreover, that both Sharif's dramaturg (myself) and choreographer (Paloma McGregor) were also Black women.

Certainly, Sharif's identificatory marker as a Black woman distinguishes her from many other LORT theater directors who have previously directed versions of Austen's work. This opportunity was made possible by Sharif's professional affiliation and friendship with Baker and Baker's knowledge of her expertise in and appreciation for the work of Jane Austen. This relation-ship, coupled with Sharif's distinguished position as Associate Artistic Direc-tor of Baltimore Center Stage – a position under the helm of (then) Artistic Director Kwame Kwei-Armah – provided the necessary support for Sharif's ordination as the world premier director of Baker's *Pride and Prejudice*.

This same prioritizing of aptitude and experience resulted in Sharif's casting of her dramaturg and choreographer. Both McGregor and I had previously worked with Sharif, securing her confidence in our value and potential to offer rich contributions to the production. Nevertheless, the racial identities of the production's director, dramaturg, and choreographer – postscripts that should exist as simple descriptive details – were not, as it turns out, quite so "simple" for some. On the contrary, I found myself hav-ing to assuage the incredulity of several potential spectators who seemed convinced of their assumption that Sharif's direction of *Pride and Prejudice* was going to be "racialized" in some way.

Though I had navigated through a few assumptive queries on my own, I was still quite surprised when I bore witness to the way in which one theater patron's persistent inquiries transformed from curious questioning into a discomforting and incriminating interrogation about the "why" and "how" of Sharif's directing an Austen adaptation. It was such a disconcerting experience for me that I felt compelled to follow-up with Sharif and ask her thoughts about "racialized casting" when it comes to artistic leadership in American theater:[3]

CARPENTER: Hana, do you remember when we had that Insights for *Pride and Prejudice*? There was a man, an older white man, that approached us at the end the event, a theater patron – or was he a board member? Do you remember?

SHARIF: Ah, yes. I think he was a guest of a board member. He does seem to be someone who is regularly at Insights. Insights is usually offered to board members and a certain donor class. And then they each can bring an invited guest. The person they usually bring is the one that is either being cultivated to be a donor or cultivated to be a board member. It's a very private invited group of people.

CARPENTER: He was subtle – at first – right?

SHARIF: Yep.

CARPENTER: I remember that it took him about three rounds before he really got to the gist of his real question, which was "What's your agenda?" And you responded by, once again, bringing focus to Jane Austen. You kept establishing just how thoroughly invested and knowledgeable you are about *Pride and Prejudice* and its context and why it is an important novel. You returned to these things, with measured poise, over and over . . .

SHARIF: Yes, I remember. There was this whole warm up. He was walking us out the door. I remember we were having a conversation together as we were exiting the building. And he came up to us. He was chit chatty. And he's walking with us. And I was wondering, "Why is this man still walking with us?" And then he said, "Well, I just wanted to ask you a couple questions." I can't remember what the leading questions were. But he got to the point when he finally said: "I'm just wondering why you didn't have any Black people in the play. It just seems like that would be the direction you would want to go." I don't remember exactly all he said, but I explained that I wanted to do a piece that honors Austen in the world at that place, at that time.

CARPENTER: He just kept insisting that if you were directing, then you should have Black actors. And you tried to talk to him about that; about what it would mean for the play, for the story onstage, to make that kind of choice.

SHARIF: Because casting it differently, casting it with actors of color, just wouldn't make any sense for the story I was trying to tell. But this year [2018], I had the great fortune of directing a production of *Sense and Sensibility* at OSF [Oregon Shakespeare Festival]. And it was an incredible opportunity to direct in a slot that a woman of color had not directed in before. At OSF, they have two shows that run for around ten months – so they run the entire season. And I directed in one of those slots. And it was another Austen piece – because, as you know, I'm passionate about Austen. And in this production there was multi-ethnic casting because it is actually part of the aesthetic of the OSF's company to always have diverse casts. I got to play with Austen's work in a world that is entirely constructed from our imaginations and not one that needed to be connected with reality in the same way. And it very much changed the tenor of the storytelling.

CARPENTER: I imagine that this brought on its own unique challenges and discoveries, yes?

SHARIF: I will say it made casting quite interesting. Even as I was casting with this team of people who are very open to this idea of "everyone can be everything," when we started to look at the characters and the motivations of the characters and the connotation of what it meant to put a person of color in a said role, suddenly it got very complex. There were characters that I was like, "There's no way in the world I'm putting a person of color in that role because of potential connotations, it could fill stereotypes that I think are very dangerous." And they felt the same way. Even in an environment where we say "everyone can be everything," you can't deconstruct it in a way that doesn't still allow us to bring all of our lived experiences to the table and all of our biases to the table. I do think that when you're going to do multi-ethnic casting then it really is a matter of color-conscious casting. You have to think about what the statement is that you're trying to make.

CARPENTER: Absolutely. But in the case of *Pride and Prejudice* at Baltimore Center Stage, the whole point was that you were intentionally focusing on the animation of Austen's world – an adaptation of it, yes, but you wanted to adhere to the rules of her world.

SHARIF: Which is why inserting someone who would not naturally have been in this environment was not the way we were going to tell the story. The Insights patron didn't seem to receive that idea. He kept trying to make sense of the fact that we were the creative team telling this story, yet the people who were in the story didn't look like us. So, there was this whole process I tried to undertake to help him understand; it was about my passion for Austen, my belief in the kind of delicate, nuanced beauty of the novel and in play. And I was trying to establish for him that I do have a scholarly authority to be able to tell this story because I actually understand her work really, really well and I have an affinity and passion for it.

CARPENTER: I think one of my many proud moments serving as your dramaturg was when, after such graceful patience, you were finally like: "Oh, and also, I'm a talented director. I got this." And it was pretty much like – drop the mic!

SHARIF: [laughs] Yes. Because the bottom line is that I'm a very talented director. And I can direct any story. And it's always stood out to me how – and this is certainly not the first time in my career that I've confronted this idea – how directors of color are only hired to direct works by or about people of color – except, occasionally, when it comes to Shakespeare. And let's be clear, I love working and directing the works of people of color. I think that some of the most brilliant new works in the American theater are coming from artists of color. There's no question about that. But what I realized early on in my career is the lack of opportunity on LORT stages for directors of color to direct work that is not ethnically specific. It's how artists of color are locked out of the top jobs as artistic directors of LORT theaters because people look at their resume and they go, "Oh, you're a really great director, and I love August Wilson. But we're not just a Black theater. And we don't know that you can direct classics. And we don't know that you can direct big shows. And we don't know if you can direct musicals other than *The Devil's Music* or something like that. I mean, your resume doesn't reflect what we're looking for – a kind of holistic artist to lead the organization." It's a catch-22, the challenges you have as a director of color. Even when you're in an environment where you're given opportunities – to have donors and board members and other people still questioning whether or not you have the ability to do the work without putting some type of extra agenda on it – it's the kind of thing that I don't believe my white colleagues face. There's an assumption that they can tell anyone's story and an assumption that we can only tell our own stories.

CARPENTER: This really feeds into what I'm trying to write about. I'm trying to think about the idea of casting, but I'm not talking about casting of actors. I'm talking about casting directors and artistic leadership. And when I first thought of this, I immediately thought of you – I thought of all your hard work, all your "auditions," and how your talent, determination, and labor has earned you some rich roles in major regional theaters. But when I think of the opportunities you've earned, it does feel like an unusual journey. You've had leadership positions that have opened up the choices and relationships to take on these things. What kinds of conversations have you had with other directors of color on this topic?

SHARIF: Very few directors have had the same level of opportunity that I've had. But this conversation about who gets to direct what – and who gets to produce – is a very real conversation. And part of it comes down to where the power to make decisions happens in our field. They happen in these artistic departments. They happen with artistic leadership. For example, when I worked at Hartford Stage – and I'm so grateful to Michael Wilson for really launching my regional theater career – when I was at Hartford, we did *Gee's Bend*, which is written by Elyzabeth Gregory Wilder. It's a beautiful play. Elyzabeth is a beautiful southern writer, a White woman. The next year when it was time to season plan, Michael said "Well, why don't you direct *Having Our Say*?" And I said "No." And also, "We shouldn't be programming it, either." And when he asked why, I explained that representation actually matters. It's not enough to say that you've diversified the bodies on stage. And I don't think it's appropriate that every time we get a Black story, it's being told through a White playwright's voice. It's okay for us to put great stories out there. But there are so many writers of color who are speaking particularly about their experience. We're producing one Black play a year. Why is that one Black play a "Black play" through a White man? At that same time, I said that I'd love to direct *Red*. And it just came back to a version of "I don't know if that's the right fit for you."

CARPENTER: But he knew of your talent and ability –

SHARIF: Yes ! I had this amazing artistic director who believed in me artistically and who believed in me as a producer, but still had this notion that was deeply engrained that you could not hire a director of color to do a play that was not inherently about their ethnic experience, their lived experience. What people don't realize is that it also limits the experience of a person of color down to only their lived experience through their skin and not the lived experience of their humanity.

In thinking through Sharif's distinction between "skin" and "humanity," I recognized more fully how apropos it was for her to direct *Pride and Prejudice* – especially in light of her insistence on "deconstructing perspectives." Sharif is a multifaceted figure: a celebrated director, playwright, producer, and theater administrator; an African American woman, a wife, a mother, and a practicing Muslim who grew up well-acquainted with Black Nationalist ideologies. While the facts of Sharif's gender, race, cultural positioning, and faith did not impact the historical context or articulated identities in Center Stage's *Pride and Prejudice*, her life experiences have undoubtedly trained her to have a nuanced understanding of the human capacity for assumptive leaps – insight that certainly informed her directorial vision. "I don't remember a time when I wasn't deconstructing who I am in the world," says Sharif. "I was encouraged to challenge what it meant to be Black, Muslim, and a woman in this society."[4] Even if one did not understand Sharif's directorial vision – or share her enthusiasm for "deconstructing perspective(s)" – one should certainly recognize that she is well versed in maneuvering through the socio-political dynamics explored within Christopher Baker's adaptation of Austen's celebrated novel. To be certain, Sharif embraced the directing of *Pride and Prejudice* as an opportunity to invite audience members to reflect on their personal pride and prejudice and, in so doing, also invited us – theater makers – to deconstruct and expand our own perspectives on casting.

Notes

1 For more on the issue of intentionality and audience interpretation, see Faedra Chatard Carpenter, "Activating the Asterisk: The Dramaturgy of Intentionality," *Journal of Dramatic Theory and Criticism*, 32.2 (2018): 129–140.

2 While Sharif was the first Black woman to lead a "mainstream" regional theatre at the time of this writing, of celebratory note is that two women of color, Maria Manuela Goyanes and Stephanie Ybarra, were later named as artistic directors of major regional theaters in 2018 (for DC's Woolly Mammoth Theater Company and Baltimore Center Stage, respectively). Happily, these appointments were followed in 2019 by that of Nataki Garrett as Artistic Director of the Oregon Shakespeare Festival.

3 Conversation by telephone, July 31, 2018.

4 "Meet the Author and the Director," *Jane Austen's Pride and Prejudice Baltimore Center Stage Program*, September 11–October 11 (2015): 8.

2 Dramaturgy as prophecy

Facing Our Truth and dramaturging the Predominantly White Institution

Scott Horstein

February 2018

Several years ago, as part of a course-related project, I interviewed the rector of a local Episcopalian church on the theme of prophecy. He described the Judeo-Christian notion of prophecy not as an act of clairvoyance but rather as an act of bearing witness. Biblical prophets such as Amos or Jeremiah proclaimed that they were not blind to the lives their fellows chose to lead. They detailed extensively what they *saw* and asserted that it *mattered*.

In his 1990 essay "The New Cultural Politics of Difference," Cornel West inhabits this same tradition, proposing a "prophetic criticism" that keeps track

> of the complex dynamics of institutional and other related power structures in order to disclose options and alternatives for transformative praxis . . . [Prophetic criticism] makes explicit its moral and political aims. It is partisan, partial, engaged, and crisis-centered, yet always keeps open a skeptical eye to avoid dogmatic traps . . . or rigid conclusions. . . . [We are] summoned by styles . . . for their profound insight, pleasures and challenges. Yet all evaluation . . . is inseparable from, though not identical or reducible to, social structural analyses, moral and political judgments and the workings of a curious critical consciousness.[1]

West's prophetic criticism feels like dramaturgy to me. Theater artists engage in two separate but related activities, sometimes simultaneously: *making* the stuff of the work itself and stepping back to *witness* the event's entirety and to imagine its impact on the community.[2] The closer one gets to opening night, the more the dramaturg's collaborators have to focus on the making. Directors have to sharpen moments and traffic patterns; performers have to solidify physical, vocal, and emotional choices; designers have to complete color and shape in space; writers have to tweak story and character details and sand down the dialogue's rough edges. In contrast, the dramaturg focuses primarily on bearing witness, assessing the overall system of moments and ideas, naming intention and meaning, and offering "options and alternatives for transformative praxis," to use West's phrase. The dramaturg enacts "I see this" as a combination of theory and practice, as an engaged, collaborative act of witness. This is not to suggest that the dramaturg is a saint among sinners. Prophecy here implies not moral superiority but ethical engagement.

In some ways, West's notion of prophecy might seem a poor fit with common dramaturgical practice. Prophetic criticism "always makes explicit its moral and political aims. It is partisan, partial, engaged, and crisis-centered." Outside of generative or ensemble modes of dramaturgy, dramaturgs tend to embrace the goals of someone else's work first and background their own aesthetic or political agendas in order to establish trust, letting personal interests and passions emerge implicitly through the interpersonal negotiation of dramaturgical process. The dramaturg's moral and political aims may appear more overtly on the borders of the process, in choice of projects, in advocacy during season selection and staffing, and in fostering discourse among the project's constituent communities.

The following is a personal account of trying to articulate moral and political aims through dramaturgy. I teach at Sonoma State University, a forty-minute drive north of San Francisco. Previous to my appointment here, I had built a personal notion of myself as someone with a certain social justice practice and credibility, through dramaturgy and directing work with artists and companies devoted to community and social justice. I had a similar notion of myself in the classroom, trying to embrace teaching as an act of community-building, a mutual honoring of student and teacher for everything they bring to the table. I do also ask students to explore the role of culture in their work, and make a point of exposing them to voices and artists along numerous vectors of culture. However, once I had begun my appointment at Sonoma State, whatever social justice practice I had or occupied a place in felt porous and inconsistent. I attributed this to the fact that my wife and I started a family, which combined with the demands of the job left me less time for outside professional work. I also attributed it to Sonoma State's identity as a PWI (Predominantly White Institution), statistically among the Whitest of the twenty-three campuses in the California State University (CSU) system[3] and struggling to address its avowed desire for "diversity." However, it now seems clear to me that my social justice practice was not so robust after all. I had not found the clarity or honesty to create a venue for prophecy, a place to "make explicit" "my moral and political aims." I offer the following as field notes on dramaturging the Predominantly White Institution and, in the spirit of West's "skeptical eye," simultaneously dramaturging the self.[4]

March 2012

In my Race, Gender, and Performance seminar, a first-year acting student, who identifies as Black, alludes to the murder of someone named Trayvon Martin and how talk of it has spread like wildfire in her community. I, the instructor, nod sagely, having not read the newspaper in days, barely understanding the reference, and afraid to expose my ignorance. I find out the following term that the student has left Sonoma State.

April–May 2014

The student organization Black Scholars United (BSU) invites an activist, the Reverend Jarrett Maupin, to speak at Sonoma State. I attend the speech. The Rev. Maupin has recently called for the expulsion of a group of White Arizona State University students who threw a "ghetto party" on Martin Luther King Day. During his visit, he meets with our university's president and also with BSU. Later, in his speech, he calls our president, a light-skinned Cuban man, an "Uncle Tom." He suggests that Black students should leave Sonoma State, because the university has shown through its actions and values that it does not want them.

The speech is effective and I feel personally accountable. What witness will I bear to this? Beyond my coursework, here in the Bay Area, in the land of Andy Lopez and Oscar Grant, how can I join with others to respond to the challenge in the speech?[5] I immediately think of *Facing Our Truth: Ten-Minute Plays on Trayvon, Race, and Privilege*. By now I know about Trayvon Martin, the seventeen-year-old teenager who was walking through his father's suburb of Sanford, Florida, on the evening of February 26, 2012, and was stalked, shot, and killed by George Zimmerman, a self-appointed vigilante neighborhood watchman. Trayvon was Black; Zimmerman is of mixed European, Latino, and African descent. A mostly White, all-female jury acquitted Zimmerman on the basis of Florida's controversial "stand your ground" law, and the verdict became a national controversy. For *Facing Our Truth*, Keith Josef Adkins, Artistic Director of the New York company The New Black Fest, commissioned eight writers and artists from different backgrounds to write ten-minute plays inspired by the Zimmerman verdict. "I told them they were not required to write about Trayvon Martin; I wanted . . . the plays to provide a safe place for ALL demographics to discuss race and privilege (in all its various manifestations)."[6]

I don't have a regular directing slot as part of my faculty appointment, but the department graciously makes room in the upcoming season for me to direct *Facing Our Truth*. I want to do the play as staged readings, with a relaxed rehearsal schedule, no memorization required, in a vocally friendly black-box space, to make the process a manageable commitment for non-theater majors from across campus. Feeling that partnership is essential, I present this proposal to BSU, as well as to the HUB (our multicultural center) and to our Office for Diversity and Inclusive Excellence, all of whom are galvanized by the prospect of building community around this theatrical event.

I realize that as dramaturg or stage or festival director I generally sign on to existing projects, whereas I've rarely conceived and built them myself, from the ground up. Building this event feels like a dramaturgical act, a way to make unified meaning out of the world as viewed from our campus.

October 2014

I'm ready to implement my grand strategy, which is to request the right to perform only the first three plays from *Facing Our Truth*. I am concerned about casting the last three, which involve a singing and guitar-playing George Zimmerman and a role for a White actress whose character becomes Black. I question my right as a White man both to direct the latter performance and to stage a rapid-fire series of lynching photos the script calls for at the climax of the play. Will I be seen as appropriating stories that are not mine to tell? Our campus partners write letters of support. I send the whole request to Keith at the New Black Fest. Keith, with whom I've worked previously, replies that the playwrights have recently decided all six plays must be performed together.

My wife, having watched me wring my hands, tells me just to do all six. I continue to worry. "But what if I can't cast it? What if I have to cancel it?" I've fallen into the "But do we have the actors for that?" trap (analyzed smartly by, among others, Brian Eugenio Herrera in his 2017 article of the same name),[7] focusing too narrowly on "diversity" as boxes to be checked on a cast list, rather than a natural outgrowth of coalition building and allyship with the communities represented on stage. I decide to go ahead with all six.

November 2014

I hold auditions for *Facing Our Truth* in a group format to emphasize the ensemble nature of the project. I can't figure out how auditioners might self-identify race as part of audition process. I decide that as long as I clearly post in advance the casting breakdown, play summaries, and script and strongly encourage the auditioners to read the scripts, then the students will understand how they might be cast. Our campus partners work hard to encourage students to try out. The auditions themselves are exciting, and the participants seem energized by the scripts and by each other. Gabriel Duran, who plays guitar and sings like Curtis Mayfield, auditions for the Zimmerman role at the encouragement of Mark Fabionar, the director of the HUB. We cast all six plays fully from our auditions. I am thrilled, and I also feel chastened for having discounted the talent and enthusiasm we have on our campus.

January–March 2015

The first ensemble meeting and read-through goes well. The eighteen students in the cast respond to the power of the plays, to a shared sense of purpose, and to belonging to an ensemble with a wide range of racial and ethnic backgrounds, roles on campus, fields of study, and performance experience. In weekly meetings the ensemble openly shares past and present experiences of race and privilege. Some students of color remember relatives who have perished in racialized violence, while others share personal stories of harassment. Still other students articulate their desires to learn from each other, to come to grips with varying senses of ignorance around these issues.

Rehearsals for each play begin. In *Night Vision* by Dominique Morisseau, a Black couple in their thirties descend into confusion, unable to agree on the race of the participants in a confusing and violent situation they have just witnessed on the street. A black hoodie, which has become a Trayvon icon, figures prominently in this play and in others. In *Some Other Kid* by A. Rey Pamatmat, a trio of teenagers grapples with moral and romantic quandaries on the eve of their high school graduation, only to have their bond ruptured by a sudden gunshot. *Colored* by Winter Miller is the big group piece, a fugue-like sequence set on a subway platform and inside a subway train, as a trio of female commuters (Blue, Green, Purple) comes into conflict with a trio of teenage male subway dancers (Pink, Red, Yellow), the dialogue hinting at some kind of racial conflict, though the significance of color in this world is intentionally ambiguous. *The Ballad of George Zimmerman*, with text by Dan O'Brien and music by Quetzal Flores, is a brief musical that mixes various folk idioms, with Zimmerman, Trayvon, and a police officer replaying in Zimmerman's mind the ritual of his encounter with Trayvon and its aftermath (Figure 2.1).

In *Dressing* by Mona Mansour and Tala Manassah, a loving mother and her son disagree over what is safe to wear when he goes out. Jump

Figure 2.1 Bria Gabor (Officer) returns the gun to Gabriel Duran (George Zimmerman) in *The Ballad of George Zimmerman*

Source: Photography credit Connor Gibson

forward, and the mother relives her son's shooting. A very dark satire ends the evening: *No More Monsters Here,* by Marcus Gardley, in which a Black psychiatrist diagnoses his White patient with "negroidphobia," then prescribes a special science-fiction hoodie that will turn her into a Black man from the "hood" for three days, at which point she will supposedly be "cured." Rebecca, the patient, dressed now as "Raheem," is eventually shot and killed but revives to find the treatment declared a success and her sense of identity in tatters.

One of the chief truths the plays dramatize is the unbearable vulnerability of being Black, of being fungible, in the formulation of radical Black scholar Orlando Patterson, of being generally dishonored, natally alienated, and the object of naked violence.[8] Kim D. Hester-Williams, a scholar of nineteenth-century literature and African American literature and film, directs *Dressing*. Lauren S. Morimoto, a kinesiology professor, former playwright, and Director for Diversity and Inclusive Excellence, directs *Some Other Kid*. Bianca Zamora, a dynamic graduating senior in Women's and Gender Studies, directs *Night Vision*.

I direct *Colored, The Ballad of George Zimmerman,* and *No More Monsters Here. Monsters* offers a good example of what's at stake in these plays. Acting major Renee Hardin plays Rebecca/Raheem in *Monsters* with an instinct for emotional truth and for comedy that serve the characters well. She also, by her own admission, doesn't know how to act "street." Despite this, my previous anxiety over casting and directing this character seems more and more off-base. At first blush Gardley's text seems to ask for the spectacle of a White actor engaging in racial impersonation, but in fact the text doesn't depend on this at all. Renee's own performance of Raheem has little overt racial inflection. The suggestion of Raheem's Blackness becomes an image for the audience to complete. One can even imagine comedy in Rebecca being very bad at "being Raheem" and the other characters not noticing.

During the rehearsal process I become aware (I don't remember how) that Rosemarie Kingfisher, who plays Greatest Grand and Ookie and is of mixed-race descent, identifies as having Native (Northern Cheyenne) and Jewish parentage.

> *GREATEST GRAND enters. She is 162, hunched over to her toes, her wig has food in it and she has a walker, which has headlights and a horn. She wears a nightgown and dirty bunny slippers that are missing one ear and an eye. . . .*
> *. . . Lights crossfade to GREATEST GRAND who is now a street thug named OOKIE. She has on baggy jeans, a plaid shirt, doo rag and some garden gloves. He sits on a hydrant.*[9]

Realizing that Rose most likely does not identify as being of African descent troubles my initial casting instincts. I wonder whether I've unwittingly authorized racial impersonation and put the actor and the show in an untenable position. How might I have addressed this as part of the casting process or made space for auditioners to identify personal goals in auditioning for a racially charged project?

Driven either by desperation or clarity, I decide to follow through on my initial instinct, that Rose's comic ability, her experiences as a woman of color, and her personal sense of political engagement honor the demands of the play, where characters continually act out of character and don Blackness and Whiteness (and masculinity and femininity) like a set of clothes. Rose's identity speaks tellingly to the many and often incendiary ways in which, as we walk around and interact in the world, we inhabit the gap between perception and self-identification. Her casting allows for an authentic engagement and allyship that I think will serve the learning goals of the student and ensemble, serve the audience, and serve the script.

At the play's climax, Rebecca's therapy for "negroidphobia" concludes when her psychiatrist, Doc, disguised as a Zimmerman-like pursuer, shoots Raheem.

> *The figure stands over Raheem and points the gun at him. Rebecca screams. We see a lightning speed projection of the following faces/ images: Medgar Evers, Emmett Till, Oscar Grant, Sean Bell, Amadou Diallo and lynched black men. . . . The figure cocks his gun, Rebecca releases a piercing scream! He shoots. Rebecca grabs her heart, she wails. She flails on the ground holding her heart. She weeps bloody murder as lights slowly rise on her. When lights come up full, the figure takes his mask off. It is DOC. He kneels, embraces REBECCA. She cries in his arms.*

(91)

I cull the images in this stage direction from internet research. Throughout the process, I advise the ensemble in advance as to when the images will be shown or projected. I try to treat the images with respect, taking time to name each victim and tell their story in the room. The play deals with the images smartly, invoking them as a sudden flash so as not to monumentalize the suffering and destruction they depict.

Performances: February–March 2015

Spirits in the green room are uproariously high. Ensemble members joke openly about race with each other. Students, family, and colleagues who attend witness a cast that is fully integrated and who have made community together. The plays and performances land with wit, joy, grief, anger, surprise, and use the stage in wildly different ways. Multiple plays repeat and ritualize Zimmerman's pursuit of Trayvon, while others place hoodies near or on actors' bodies, the signification of the hoodie wavering between quotidian unremarkability and a curse.

A faculty colleague, who identifies as White, relates to me that during the performance of *Dressing* she is so overcome by grief that students on either side of her, both strangers, silently take her hands. In facilitated dialogue after each show, Black students and students of color in general speak to the plays' depictions of the lived realities of race, allowing for a frankness of dialogue with White folks that may be rare on this campus. I visit a colleague's classroom, where a Black student confesses her thoughts as she rooted for Rebecca at the end of *Monsters*. "I was thinking, 'Please don't be Black!'"

At one of the dialogues Rose Kingfisher exclaims, "I want people to know my racc!" I assume that her comment expresses a discomfort she feels in playing her roles in *Monsters*, but she doesn't elaborate. In a later post-mortem with the ensemble, Kim D. Hester-Williams, who directed *Dressing*, is moved by Rose's growth in the role of Greatest Grand, declaring that on the second weekend of the show, "Granny was here!" Rose has since graduated; I had never asked her about these moments until I had coffee with her three weeks ago, in preparation for writing these notes. Rose surprised me by saying she never felt uncomfortable with the roles. "I knew there must have been some reason why you cast me in the part, and I wanted to honor it."[10]

May 2015–February 2018

At Commencement 2015, student speaker Sasha-Rose Wroten, who attended the plays and is Black, says she is proud to be graduating from an institution that produced *Facing Our Truth*. The plays help launch an equity and inclusion initiative in our department, a continuing series of conversations, guest artist residencies, performances, and workshops, exploring new strategies for casting, recruiting, programming, curriculum, and hiring. In the summer of 2016, a new university president, a woman of color, brings a new atmosphere of transparency and accountability, as well as an overt dedication to social justice.

Facing Our Truth makes me feel whole as an artist and an academic, perhaps for the first time since beginning my tenure at this PWI. If building a prophetic act of social justice means "making explicit" my "moral and political aims," *Facing Our Truth* has helped me learn to make them central to the artistic process. Prophecy, the act of saying "I see this," is dramaturgy; it is both active and reflective, in Cornel West's words, "always keeping open a skeptical eye to avoid dogmatic traps . . . or rigid conclusions." The fragility and porousness that once so worried me in activating my social justice practice now appear as challenges to humility, a proper acknowledgment of how much I have to learn.

Notes

1 Cornel West, "The New Cultural Politics of Difference," 4–32, in *Keeping Faith: Philosophy and Race in America* (New York: Routledge, 1993), 23–24.
2 For a fascinating, next-generation riff on ethics and prophecy in the Black radical tradition, see Stefan Harvey and Fred Moten, *The Undercommons: Fugitive Planning & Black Study* (New York: Minor Compositions, 2013), 93, 130–131. Fred Moten offers the following formulation of prophecy: "You talk about being

able to be in two places at the same time, but also to be able to be two times in the same place. . . . That double-sense, that double-capacity: to see what's right in front of you and to see through that to what's up ahead of you" (131).

3 "SSU Enrollment by Campus and Ethnic Group," Fall 2015. Available online at www.calstate.edu/as/stat_reports/2015-2016/feth02.htm.

4 In this chapter I name and capitalize "White" and "Black" rather than use, say, "Caucasian" or "African American." Many different kinds of terminology for race can be useful in different discussions. The naming and capitalizing of "White" and "Black" is a nod to Whiteness and Blackness as racial realities, not simply as names for ethnicity or for identity but, in keeping with usage in cultural studies, as structural positions within social formations.

5 Andy Lopez was a thirteen-year-old Latino boy shot and killed by a police officer in Santa Rosa, California, on October 23, 2013. Oscar Grant was an eighteen-year-old Black man who was shot and killed by transit police on January 1, 2009, in Oakland, California (Grant's murder was depicted in Ryan Coogler's 2013 film *Fruitvale Station*). Both cases led to large, ongoing protests and played a major role in the rising national discourse on police brutality against people of color.

6 Conversation by e-mail, February 2015.

7 Brian Eugenio Herrera, "'But Do We Have the Actors for That?' Some Principles of Practice for Staging Latinx Plays in a University Theatre Context," 23–35, *Theatre Topics*, 27.1 (March 2017).

8 As discussed in Frank B. Wilderson III, *Red, White, and Black: Cinema and the Structure of US Antagonisms* (Durham, NC: Duke University Press, 2010), 14.

9 Marcus Gardley, "No More Monsters Here," 79–93, in *Facing Our Truth: 10-Minute Plays on Trayvon, Race, and Privilege* (New York: Samuel French, 2015), 86, 89.

10 Conversation (telephone interview), February 16, 2018.

3 The dramaturgy of the classroom

Awele Makeba

Irving Goffman, often called the father of dramaturgy, suggested in the twentieth century that life is dramaturgy – that elements of human interaction are dependent upon time, place, and audience. Perhaps nowhere do you feel this more intensely than as a drama teacher in a busy, under-funded high school, where you are presented with ninth through twelfth grade students who are historically underserved, often experiencing more than one of the Adverse Childhood Experiences (ACEs) together with toxic stress. Trauma-informed care is therefore key to my practice. My students range massively in terms of measurable "competencies" (for example, 51% of incoming freshmen lag multiple grade levels behind in reading and math). Additionally, many teens commute for over an hour to get to school, some are family caretakers for younger siblings, and many others hold down after-school and weekend jobs.

We at Skyline High School are categorized as a Title I school, with 75% of our 1,800 students receiving free or reduced-priced lunch. Every year in the last five years, 25 colleagues have left and new staff have filled those positions. I've had a new incoming school principal every single year. For the first time since my own hiring in 2013, I now feel, in 2020, as though I have co-directors who are able to support the performing arts.

Each year, before we ever get to the direction of my students' studies or to what I plan to direct for the stage, there are challenges that need to be addressed. I need first to assess what the student interactions may be, where the students may come from (each student has a constantly thrumming and shifting backstory), and how I can direct this group of young people to think of their own lives dramaturgically (*Who am I? What is my relation to my home, to the students around me, to perceived slights or misunderstandings?*) This metadramatic connection – through which students examine their lives in terms of ongoing "staged" interactions – is very important to their understanding of what theater is and does. And here's another factor:

many of the students to whom I teach theater studies have never seen a professional play. (Our geographical location in the east Oakland hills, the family budgets, our distance from Bay Area Rapid Transit, and our AC Public Transit system do not lend themselves to matinee fieldtrips, and a charter bus costs $700 for a two-hour trip.) How do you teach drama and theater-making to students who have never seen professional theater?

In answer to this last question, it is important to begin by helping students to see the dramaturgical associations mentioned earlier. And in order to scaffold this part, I forge connections. My preparation for the upcoming Skyline fall theater class begins at the very beginning of the summer holiday. Over the last three summers I've done an externship (teacher self-guided inquiry with an industry partner) at the California Shakespeare Theater. I've also completed a teacher workshop at the Oregon Shakespeare Festival, as well as shadowing my students on scholarship at the American Conservatory Theatre Young Conservatory program in partnership with the Education Department, my other community partner. I forge and facilitate connections with professionals – dramaturgs, fight coaches, choreographers, actors, designers – all of whom can be my future guest artists, offer master classes, or allow my students to come see a dress rehearsal (for the actors, an improvised fresh audience – so the benefit goes both ways). I have to gauge these professionals' availability, realizing that the nature of contract employment means that they may suddenly be in rehearsal when I had planned for them to come to class. In other words, I have to create backup and flexibility.

I concentrate on all aspects of production, using a through-line of dramaturgy. Together with Philippa Kelly, I created a curriculum for programs that we were able to get sponsorship for: *Making Shakespeare Real and Relevant* and *Making Theater Real and Relevant*. Through support from foundations,[1] we were able to set up curriculum components for the classroom featuring dramaturgy and, with the input of resident artists, to "build out" these curricular components into fully-fledged performances, complete with set design, lighting, costume, even concessions.

How did the classroom aspect work? In our exploration of *Hamlet*, for example, we examined issues of integrity, loyalty, social justice, and individuality, in relationship to organizational culture, as well as seven themes that we called "key knowledge" – death, family, madness, language, spying, revenge, politics. And, as our umbrella concept, we examined the questions: *Who am I? What legacy does my family give to or impose on me, and how much responsibility do I have to honor this legacy? To avenge a father's injustice? If I think of myself as Hamlet, how does my situation look from the perspective of another son and daughter who have lost their father – ironically, **because** of me?* Free-writes were important, as well as

Socratic seminars, circle brainstorming, and adoption of individual role perspectives within roundtable (minus the table – on-the-floor) discussions. Shakespeare's *Hamlet* became our canvas for learning. *Define yourself in a world that keeps saying no. Define what is and feels real in a world framed by negatives. Compose actions in juxtaposition to thought.*

Building on this fall study curriculum, we created a spring social justice performance, taking themes from *Hamlet* (self-identity, opposition, loyalty, legacy, self-actualization) and applying them to transformative figures from contemporary American history, making a play text that engaged with and described these figures' struggles toward individuation. Called *Teens Igniting Change in the World*, this production was based on the theme of restorative justice. Each story within the production was researched, brainstormed, discussed, written, and dramaturged by a small group of students, and I directed the composite.

Romeo and Juliet began with some similar approaches to the *Hamlet* curriculum component – *How far does my family define me? How much loyalty do I owe to a history I don't even understand, and how can I move through this legacy toward individuation?* In *Romeo and Juliet*, the cost of the lovers' individuation is fatal. This led us to study many contemporary themes of familial and gender constraint, impulse control, the power of language to define who we are, and its power also to release emotion that is, in a sense, not just to be expressed, but to be newly understood.

Philippa and I built in Essential Questions (EQs), Driving Questions (DQs), and Enduring Understandings (EUs) using the Understanding by Design curriculum model. Here is an example of each:

EQ: *How does my engagement with the play and character serve my understanding and agency in the world via a deeper and richer stage enabled by historical distance?* In other words, how does theater allow for the twin engines of empathy and estrangement?

DQ: *What issues, themes, and ambiguities are provoked by the particular production we are watching or the production we are building?*

EU: *To feel and imagine; to think and expand; to understand the complexities in students' own lives in relationship to Hamlet their contemporary, to Romeo and Juliet, Tybalt, Polonius (yes, even an elderly man!), all of whom can be the students' contemporaries?*

Into our curriculum components we built language analyses of text; we used Philippa's annotations as a scaffold for students' own explanations, appointing students as wordsmiths, and we considered the role of verse in unfolding and meaning and expressing the paradoxes that human beings can and do hold in navigating everyday life.

For my classes at Skyline High, each year is different. Each year has a new set of students. As mentioned earlier, much of my work is done outside of the classroom, in contexts in which I'm not paid, except by the spark of recognition, excitement, sometimes passion and challenge, that I see in a student's eyes or body language. Because of the funding inequities at my school at the district level, teaching at a low-income high school is not for the faint-hearted. I often decide to pay for materials myself and drive students to and from rehearsals; I have housed students with me, and I've assisted in identifying temporary shelters for a family; buying groceries and back-to-school clothes; paying cell phone bills; repairing cracked cell phone screens; buying food for after-school production rehearsals; paying for Ubers to transport students home, to work, and to their therapist appointments; and paying for a rental car to transport students from Oakland to the Oregon Shakespeare Festival in Ashland, Oregon. I've also raised $55,000 for my students to perform via invitation in the American High School Theatre Festival at Festival Fringe 2017 in Edinburgh, Scotland, which included taking master classes, attending performances, and an international performing arts college fair (they won Best Production). Why do I do this, you might ask? Because of what happens when we make theater, because, as I will describe in detail later, I believe that theater can transform young lives and carry this transformation to the next generation.

***

Why this play now? This is a question that guides students' inquiry, their lines of research, and their relationships with the rest of the ensemble and the audience. *Xtigone, SNAKES, Prospect High: Brooklyn, Every 48 Hours, Hamlet, Teens Igniting Change in the World, Romeo and Juliet,* and *A Place to Belong* were chosen for production or scene study for our exploration of the universal and fundamental qualities of what it means to be human and to activate a relationship between critical performance pedagogy and the larger themes embedded in civics and history. We have explored real-world issues and themes that my teens grapple with daily at school: school climate and culture, issues of identity formation (our chosen and imposed identities), safety and acceptance, othering, bullying, implicit bias, racial profiling, race and violence in America, the school-to-prison pipeline and mass incarceration, police brutality, crossing social borders to build community and making amends to repair the harm as best as possible, LGBTQ acceptance, immigration policy and undocumented youth, displacement and gentrification, teen activism, and disrupting systems of inequality or calling the injustice by its name if we cannot remove it. I utilize a pedagogical framework for students to develop and analyze a critical understanding of how a complex system of racial inequality and inequity is perpetuated in our school and community, and, via theater, we work to generate alternatives for change. So, the plays in my curriculum offer stories of resistance, challenging stock stories that reinforce status quo power relations.

It is my hope to inspire my students and audience members to constantly push for change, and through thoughtful analysis of history and culture we strive to examine the roots of racism, power and economics, bias, privilege, and institutional and structural racism in our educational system, shaping all of this into an understanding of the given circumstances of characters in the world of the play. This brings me to a quote I've always pondered from the brilliant scholar W.E.B. DuBois. DuBois wrote of "double consciousness" in his 1903 publication *The Souls of Black Folk*, describing the individual sensation of feeling as though your identity is divided into several parts, making it difficult or impossible to have one unified identity: "it is a peculiar sensation, this double consciousness, this sense of always looking at one's self through the eyes of others, of measuring one's soul by the tape of a world that looks on in amused contempt and pity."[2] Or, alternatively put by one of my favorite dramaturgs, "One is always looking at oneself through the eyes of others" (Dr. Philippa Kelly).[3]

Notes

1 The Walter and Elise Haas Foundation (2017 and 2018) and the California Arts Council (2018).
2 W.E.B. Du Bois, *The Souls of Black Folk* (New York: Dover Publications, 1903).
3 Quote from Dr. Philippa Kelly, Skyline High School class, 2019.

Figure 3.1 Awele Makeba
Source: Photography credit Briana Guillory

Section Two

Taking up positions – playwright/dramaturg

4 The dramaturgy of Black culture

The Court Theatre's productions of August Wilson's Century Cycle

Martine Kei Green-Rogers

As artists from historically under-represented groups have always known – and mainstream American theater is just realizing – representation is everything. The tools of dramaturgy must be utilized to ensure that the story unfolding onstage represents the complex nuances of the Black experience, rather than unintentionally playing into biases and stereotypes that can plague theatrical (and other artistic) representations of this experience.

In 2010, I dramaturged my first production with Court Theatre, *Homei*, by Samm-Art Williams, directed by Ron OJ Parson. That production was the beginning of a now eight-year relationship in which I have come to dramaturg most of the plays that Parson directs at Court Theatre. There are numerous reasons why Parson continues to request me as his dramaturg when he directs at this theater, including my background as a classical dramaturg, my PhD research in African American Theater, and, in no small part, my jovial nature in a rehearsal hall. However, I think the most important reason (at least in the beginning) has been Parson's desire to cultivate working relationships with Black artists so that his production teams at Court Theatre are racially diverse.

Thus far, I have dramaturged the following plays for Parson at Court: *Home, The Mountaintop, Seven Guitars, Waiting for Godot, Gem of the Ocean, Blues for an Alabama Sky, Five Guys Named Moe*, and *Radio Golf*. All of these plays have their separate challenges and relationships to Black culture, yet there is something special for us both about the productions of August Wilson's work.[1] Essentially, these productions are connected by a writer's oeuvre and, more importantly, by a larger historical structural frame (their place in Wilson's Century Cycle). The connection allows for Parson and myself to live in the cultural context of Wilson's oeuvre, sharing a cultural background that is important to the storytelling of the play – since we are both Black artists – and highlighting the significance of Court's commitment to producing Wilson's works in a way that honors the playwright's Century Cycle through our shared process of discovery.[2]

My first Wilson production with Parson, *Seven Guitars*, took place during Court Theatre's 2013–14 season. The production ran from January 9, 2014 until February 16, 2014. Starring Chicago Black actor "royalty" such as Kelvin Roston, Jr. (Floyd Barton), Felicia Fields (Louise), Allen Gilmore (Hedley), and Jerod Haynes (Canewell), from the very first rehearsal, it was obvious that this production had the potential to be a celebration of Black culture (in terms of the production's representation of 1940s Pittsburgh and in the gathering of Black artists who came together in 2014 to build this production).

What is important to note about the production, however, is its position within the larger 2013–14 season at Court Theatre. This particular season was unconventional for Court Theatre in terms of the variety of actors' bodies and playwrights' stories onstage. As a theater whose mission is to "make a lasting contribution to classic American theater by expanding the canon of translations, adaptations, and classic texts," this mission had often translated into work done by dead White men.[3] Yet, Court Theatre opened the 2013–14 season with *The Mountaintop* (also directed by Parson), followed by *An Iliad, Seven Guitars, Water by the Spoonful*, and *M. Butterfly*. When compared to previous seasons, such as 2012–13's *Jitney, James Joyce's "The Dead," Skylight, Proof, The Misanthrope*, and *Tartuffe* and 2011–12's *Spunk, An Iliad, Invisible Man*, and *Angels in America*, the leaders at Court in the following (2013–14) season seemed to gain a new understanding of the theater's mission, dedicated to "reviv[ing] lost masterpieces; illuminat[ing] familiar texts; explor[ing] the African American theatrical canon; and discover[ing] fresh, modern classics."[4] Essentially, leadership at the Court Theatre realized while planning their 2013–14 season that they could fulfill their stated mission and embrace a better spirit of inclusivity by widening their racial and ethnic demographics with the playwrights they chose.

For this reason, many of my conversations with Parson as we prepared for *Seven Guitars* focused on the impact of Wilson's narrative within such a season. What does it mean to have two shows in a season in which Black men are killed (onstage or no) as part of the story/historical legacy, especially as we are the artists responsible for the storytelling in both shows?[5] What does Wilson's story mean when compared to the stories of Hwang and Hudes in that season, and do we need to use our story to create an intercultural dialogue between the variety of bodies being represented in the season?

These questions manifested into action within the rehearsal and production process in a few different veins. First and foremost, we wanted to use the joy and community found in Wilson's depiction of the late 1940s as a way to temper the violence that would eventually come to light in the script. It was important to us to use the places in which music factored into Wilson's dramaturgy as opportunities to create intratextual and extra-textual storytelling moments. Parson and I felt that it was imperative that the production not mire itself in the impending death of Floyd but rather celebrate his life and experiences in the play and use that as the energy to move us toward the question of *why* Floyd dies. In addition, both Parson and I as artists tend to resist productions about the Black experience (especially when directed by those outside of the cultural context who have not actively worked on their cultural competency about this experience) that bog and "marinate" the storytelling in the aesthetic narrative of the "down and out" Black person. We believe that in even the direst of circumstances, Black people have found ways to exude joy, and we feel that Wilson invites dramaturgy that thrives on that premise – the intentionality of expressing joy in all contexts, perhaps most importantly through pain.

As a result, the songs in the show took on a life of their own.[6] These moments became about the performance of the music but also about the joy the characters had in playing their instruments with each other. Although this is a normative part of Wilson's dramaturgy, what was different in our approach was that we asked how we could bring the audience into the joy, as opposed to the audience being voyeurs who bear witness to this moment. We included popular dances and forms of choreography to space the actor/dance in such a way that the audience was embraced within the dance rather than sitting on its fringes and prone to exoticizing the actors onstage. Much of this chorographical aesthetic is built into a soul line dance[7] – which allows the audience to become and remain invested in the events of the dance.

Second, we consulted with historians at the University of Chicago to discuss Hedley's Shamanistic practices within Wilson's play. By discussing his actions with social and cultural experts, we aimed to create a faithful representation of these actions, rooted in a sincere and authentic practice. As a result, such moments functioned, dramaturgically, as a way of illustrating how and why (in a very visceral manner) Hedley would think that the money he stumbled upon was meant for him and that Floyd was interfering in his destiny.

Additionally, we used the dramaturgical program note as a way to think through the context and representation of Black life and to frame the show that the audience would see. This particular production would create the pilot for a system that Parson and I have continued to use to frame audience experiences. Typically, before going into rehearsal we sit and discuss the play in a casual way. As we chat about the play, we record the conversation, and that becomes the basis for the program note. In preparation for *Seven*

Guitars, for example, we waxed poetical about the themes, the moments that resonated the most for us, and the way Wilson masterfully incorporates moments of Pittsburgh's history into his plays – but this conversation also served as an informal check-in for us about the storytelling process itself. From the conversation we shared, I settled on the title "Wilson, Black Theater and *Seven Guitars*: Discussing the Importance of African American Voices" for the program note. The note began as follows:

> In 1996, August Wilson gave a definitive talk at the Theatre Communications Group (TCG) conference. This speech became a watershed experience for Black theater. The reason? Wilson took to task the space, or lack thereof, that white theaters and its supporters/funders have given to Black theater.
>
> In light of the upcoming production of *King Hedley II* (Wilson's "continuance" of the story of several characters from *Seven Guitars*) by a fellow Chicago theater, Congo Square, in March 2014, I thought it would be a good idea to discuss Wilson's thoughts on Black theater, how he felt about majority-run institutions doing Black theater, and how those thoughts connect to this production of *Seven Guitars*.[8]

We felt that the spirit of Wilson's speech, coupled with the city-wide conversation on Wilson's work occurring via these two Chicago theaters – one with a Black diasporic focus and the other's (Court's) classics-centric focus – would create great fodder for the audience to contemplate. Our conversation engaged with and brought the audience into the question of what Wilson's legacy means for the production of Black work on American stages and the importance of inter-city theatrical conversations that highlight issues of representation, bias, access, diversity, inclusion, justice, etc. in the field.

This framing conversation had noticeable effects on the production. The themes and ideas that emerged as the most important to us and which we thereafter wove into the production were reflected in reviewers' discussions of the show. For example, some talked about it as a production and as a contextual event that marked the play's history in Chicago. Zach Freeman of the *New City Stage* stated:

> '*Seven Guitars*' first opened in 1995 at the Goodman Theatre as Wilson was literally finishing the lines, but on the night I attended this production, today's Court Theatre audience – within walking distance of the first Black President's house, witnessing the current rebuilding south of the Midway and the integrated neighborhoods of Hyde Park – was

tapping their feet to the beat, chuckling to themselves repeatedly about the nuance of the inner Black familial, and shaking their heads to the straight-talking inner-workings of growing up a southern transplant, as a poor Black who "gets it both ways." Wilson gets the language right.[9]

Freeman continued:

> What we hear . . . with Wilson . . . is how each of these small, seemingly unimportant moments adds up, layer by layer, to the textured history of an entire people. Parson clearly understands that, which goes a long way toward explaining why the Court's productions of Wilson's plays are making unforgettable history of their own.[10]

Chris Jones of the *Chicago Tribune* also picked up on the tone we had striven to create in the production, acknowledging the "relaxed, playful quality of Ron OJ Parson's series of Wilson productions at the Court Theatre."[11] Jones' review continued, "You don't have to be any particular kind of person to understand these characters' worries over risk and safety. We all struggle with it daily. But the point of *Seven Guitars*, I think, is that Wilson is saying that you've still got to make your music. And at Court, so they do."[12]

Knowing the importance of our conversations to the production and seeing also that reviewers had understood the mode of storytelling that Parson and I attempted to foster through our collaboration, as we embarked on our next Wilson production – Court's 2015 *Gem of the Ocean* – we considered ways to keep this tone and mode of storytelling alive as we moved forward into production. We knew we needed to embrace and celebrate *Gem*'s preeminence as the first of Wilson's Century Cycle (it is set in 1904). Therefore, we began collaborating even earlier than we had in the past – with myself attending conversations about the world of the play with designers prior to the first production meeting. In many ways, we continued on the path we had established in *Seven Guitars*, yet I wanted to make sure that we were always discussing the plot of this play in relationship to other plays in the cycle. Therefore, I created a handout that I referred to often during the rehearsal process, outlining the connections between characters and places within the Century Cycle.

Early in the process we facilitated conversations among members of the design team to think through the visual and aural representations of historical and mythological Black experience onstage – the excursion to the "City of Bones" in the text. We wanted to imagine what that would look like and how we could use the resources available at the University of

Chicago to create this moment. We called upon the same experts from the scholarly community who had helped us with *Seven Guitars* – so that they in effect became ongoing collaborators in our continued conversation – and relayed their ideas to the choreographer for the production (who was the same choreographer we used for *Seven Guitars*). We crafted a moment that resembled a dance used to conjure the ancestors and spirits of the middle passage while also staying just shy of faithfully recreating those dances – since we did not want to *actually* conjure (and potentially anger) the ancestors while performing the piece! We shared this with the scholarly community at the University of Chicago, who appreciated our care and finesse in creating the moment. We revisited the same conversational process for the program notes and included talkbacks in that process.

In August 2018, Parson and I collaborated on *Radio Golf* at Court Theatre. Many of the materials I created and found for *Gem of the Ocean* were useful also for this production, since it is the other bookend to Wilson's Century Cycle. In some ways, we returned to the process that we used for previous productions, asking the questions that matter in terms of Black representation for this play. How does the representation of Black wealth and prosperity affect the themes in this production? What is Wilson saying about the effects of gentrification on Black neighborhoods? We planned a golfing lesson for all of the actors in the production as part of our rehearsal process, and used what we learned and felt from that excursion to process how Black bodies are perceived in different public venues: once again, we pushed for a kind of storytelling that could challenge and unravel old "truths" and trajectories.

Notes

1 The production of *Waiting for Godot* featured an African American cast.
2 I need to acknowledge here that there are two productions of Wilson's work at Court that I did not dramaturg – his production of *Jitney* in 2012 and his production of *Ma Rainey's Black Bottom* in 2009.
3 Available online at www.courttheatre.org/about/.
4 Ibid.
5 Parson and I collaborated on *The Mountaintop* by Katori Hall earlier in the season.
6 Please see an example of this in the following video: https://youtu.be/Jc_SUpZUV6g.
7 *The Washington Post* defines this term as "line dancing to R&B and hip-hop songs." Victoria St. Martin, "With a Kick and a Spin, a Sudden Surge in Soul Line Dancing," *The Washington Post*, June 26, 2016.
8 Martine Green-Rogers, "Wilson, Black Theatre and *Seven Guitars*: Discussing the Importance of African American Voices," available online at https://issuu.com/footlights/docs/court-sevenguitars.

9 Zach Freeman, "Review: Seven Guitars/Court Theatre," *New City Stage*, February 1, 2014.
10 Ibid.
11 Chris Jones, "'Guitars' Has a Relaxed and Playful Vibe," *Chicago Tribune*, January 20, 2014.
12 Ibid.

5 Embodied dramaturgy

The development of the indigenous play, *The Patron Saint of the Lost Children*

Izumi Ashizawa, with Ajuawak Kapashesit

In addition to my regular directorial work as an intercultural practitioner of devised theater, I have had the opportunity to serve as production dramaturg for major national and international commercial productions. While my task as dramaturg varies from production to production, most of my experiences have been framed by the institutional structure of the commercial theater where the hierarchical code of the creative process is rather inflexible. In these scenarios, dramaturgical voices are not always used to the fullest level to enhance the quality of the production. In some cases, a dramaturg with a racial minority background is summoned to satisfy the production's diversity requirement and is neither expected nor invited to engage fully in the creative conversation, nor even to contribute specific cultural knowledge.

Therefore, I was thrilled to have the opportunity explore a completely unorthodox approach to dramaturgy alongside the indigenous playwright Ajuawak Kapashesit. We wanted to deconstruct dramaturgy's conventional hierarchies and methodologies in order to create and establish a shared language for *The Patron Saint of the Lost Children*.

The play development process for *The Patron Saint of the Lost Children* took place from July 16–26, 2018, during the convening of the National Institute for Directing and Ensemble Creation in Minnesota. During this convention, organized by the Pangea World Theatre and Art2Action, Ajuawak and I were teamed up as mentor/mentee partners. Since we live in different states, the majority of our communication to that point had been online, and those discussions tended to focus on theoretical aspects of the creative process such as conceptual and thematic analysis. Once we were in the same place, we were able to begin the hands-on development of Ajuawak's artistic craft. I asked him at the beginning what he needed in order to develop his play; he answered, "physical elements." As a Japanese practitioner of devised physical theater, I envisioned using my experimental physical routine techniques as a tool to develop his play. Thus, the embodied dramaturgy process – a process that formed a union of two cultures – took root.

The Patron Saint of The Lost Children is a period drama that takes place in and around St. Anastasia's, a fictional Indian boarding school typical of the Boarding School Era within the United States, when young indigenous children were taken away from their homes and taught Euro-American subject matter in order to fulfill the colonialist mission of Native American assimilation. Two of these Native students flee the school: Susan/Miigwaansikwe, who hopes to go home, and George/Waazhashk, who hopes to escape his past. They are followed by a determined priest, one of the school's former wards, who evokes the lonely spirit of the nearby forest. Combining aspects of film noir, historical writing, and magical realism, this play explores the guilt, horror, and despair of the Boarding School Era through the experiences both of its perpetrators and its victims, aiming to leave audiences with a sliver of hope for the future borne out of this painful part of history.

Initially, my single objective was to support my fellow playwright in the most effective way I could. Since there were no hierarchically-imposed restrictions on our collaborative partnership, the creative environment was flexible enough to allow us to be spontaneous. We were able to intentionally subvert conventional processes in order to create our own style of dramaturgy. We wanted, by the end of our time together, to map our developmental process in the hope that besides tracking the evolution of our project it might also provide a scaffolding for other embodied-dramaturgy processes.

First, we agreed that non-verbal elements would be crucial to our process. I came up with the idea of applying the physical devising techniques that I usually employ to make dramaturgical support materials. Without explaining in too much detail, I asked Ajuawak to jump into a dual experimental movement exercise (Figure 5.1).

When I first read his play, I got the impression that the relationship between the two children grew too abruptly to convince me of the plausibility of a character called George who performs his final act of self-sacrifice. The playwright saw how this looked through my eyes. Thus, I focused on helping him to envision, via experimental physical exercises, the development of the relationship between the two characters. I intentionally avoided specificity in my physical rendering. This type of process required us to trust each other.

Our experimental exercise began with a physical embodiment of the development in the characters' relationship. We explored the range of physical distances between our bodies and improvised how we would each react to distance as physical and emotional sensation. We repeated the same exercise until it settled into a distance that mapped our way to what we saw as

Figure 5.1 Izumi Ashizawa, with Ajuawak Kapashesit, in rehearsal for *The Patron Saint of the Lost Children*

Source: Photography credit Bruce Silcox

the conclusion of the characters' relationship. At the end of the exercise, we intentionally avoided talking about the experience and moved onto the next set of exercises. Thus, physical sensation and intuition – rather than conversation and deliberation – led us to different levels of understanding.

We ended the session with a very simple exercise: becoming children. All I asked of Ajuawak was to hold my hand and never let go so that we could become children together. We giggled, rolled around, and teased each other for about fifteen minutes until the two of us ended up lying down and falling asleep holding each other's hands. We then immediately repeated the same exercise, but this time we did so "as" the characters in the play and with the plot in mind. The simple and playful exercise that we had done just moments ago blossomed into structured storytelling. Throughout the exercises, we prevented ourselves from speaking. This enabled the progression of the relationship to emerge clearly. The moment when Ajuawak finally let my hand go became a clear signal for his character's sacrifice.

After the session, we briefly talked about our first impressions of the exercises, focusing on describing sensation rather than analytical discussion: I wanted to give Ajuawak the space to process and digest alone. This is typical of Japanese methodologies in artistic practice: before processing the experience through logos, let the physical sensation lead to an answer. Since my childhood, I have practiced different genres of Japanese arts in which artistic rituals are physically embodied. This is a practical legacy that I inherited from my ancestors. It is not a coincidence that my practice harmonizes with Ajuawak's form of play development. His Ojibwe tribe also has a long history of embodied ritual practice. Two artists with two different cultural legacies were able to discover a shared artistic language (Figure 5.2).

In our session the following day, we experimented with two simple songs that each of us had brought. Instead of using verbal language, I asked Ajuawak to tell me a story using his song. We explored a variety of intonations and gestures, repeating the same exercise with different interpretations for approximately half an hour. Then, I asked him to repeat the exercise in the manner of the two different characters in his play. A new level of character relationship emerged. The intimacy and protective nature that had not previously existed in the character of George began to grow. It was a clear moment in which we seemed to have brought into focus the full set of materials from these two consecutive days of embodied experimental dramaturgy.

Figure 5.2 The Patron Saint of the Lost Children, embodied dramaturgy

Source: Photography credit Bruce Silcox

We decided to structure all of the experimental materials into a cohesive narrative. I gave this task of structural organization to Ajuawak and let him direct me. In this process, I transitioned from a dramaturg to an actress performing in front of the audience that we had gathered for the event. It was my aim that this embodied directorial practice would lead Ajuawak further on his journey for developing the script. Our presentation time was limited to five minutes. In this time, we managed to summarize all of the experimental materials and to create a condensed version of the play with only two songs and no spoken words. The audience shared afterwards that the progression of the characters' relationship felt very much present in this performance. Ajuawak then began to revise his play. Following is his statement on our embodied dramaturgical experimentation:

I had begun working on this story in late 2017. Upon completion of the first draft of the play, I sent it out to many writers and performers I personally know for input. Much of the advice I was given was quite helpful in my rewriting. However, working with Izumi Ashizawa on this piece during the Pangea World Theatre and Art2Action's National Institute for Directing and Ensemble Creation (which convened in the Summer of 2018) helped me to actually see some of the characters come to life; and through this I noticed flaws and inconsistencies that did not occur to me via other feedback. For example, I had intended to make the character of Susan, the young girl in the play, younger. Once Izumi and I began to work on this story as a performance offering for the convention, Izumi helped me to understand the age of the character more clearly. Susan is a child, still quite innocent, and able to communicate with the spirit in the forest. In my writing, she had come off as far more adult and at times even maternal, which is inappropriate for this character in order to be in alignment with her staged age and personal outlook. A similar issue arose in the character of George, the teenage boy, whom I myself performed during our rehearsals and in our performance. In the performance, I realized that my interpretation of George on the stage did not align with his character on the page. The George whom I had written as a person was greatly influenced by film noir protagonists such as Humphrey Bogart. Thus, his attitude and how he speaks according to the page is often more mature than he would be as a staged boy.

My work on the piece with Izumi included an exercise in which we performed just as children rather than as any particular characters. This allowed us to play with youthful exuberance and without inhibition – it served Susan's character well and influenced the mannerisms of George who is, after all, still a child himself. Further, our work included a process of launching each other across the space. This was more physically interesting to watch on stage and also led to an important metaphor about their world. The characters themselves are on a voyage and it becomes clear that they will progress much more effectively if they work together. The physicality accelerated their relationship as both friends and fellow escapees, and I am excited to elaborate this aspect further on in the piece. It is also another example of the details I found, and was able to address, in my work while collaborating with Izumi in this way.

Our revisions were made possible because two artists with two different backgrounds in embodied, ritualistic practice found a common artistic language: an unorthodox approach to dramaturgy that became a collaborative form of generation and strength for artists who had experienced our own voices, in western rehearsal rooms, as somewhat exoticized and marginalized by our colleagues. I have practiced traditional Japanese Noh theater, traditional painting, calligraphy, tea ceremony, and flower arrangement: all traditional Japanese arts consist of "kata," or the concept of forms. And through the physical forms, the artists explore an internal world. I call it an outside-in approach, as opposed to the western inside-out approach. This philosophical concept, embedded in my body, is probably the most valuable influence on my creative process.

I believe that embodied dramaturgy allows artists to map a shared space together. I will observe what the playwright is doing, identifying what might be the best physical experimental exercises us to try. For Ajuawak's play, I determined the paths that we took in order to release and add specificity to the characters of George and Susan. For another playwright, there will be different kinds of outside-in exercises. Embodied dramaturgy creates an original dramaturgical language, igniting an important method for revision and generation.

6 The name (isn't a) game

New explorations in trans applied theater

Finn Lefevre

"Hi, I'm Finn," I say to the person in front of me, poised to begin our first exercise. We shake hands, and suddenly the rules of the game change. I am now Castriela, the name of the person whose hand I just shook, and she is Finn. We find a new partner and introduce ourselves with these new monikers, shake hands, and instantly trade names again. The game continues, until everyone has introduced themselves to everyone else, regardless of which name they used. Then we freeze and are told to find our names amongst the mixed-up menagerie of others. But I don't find my name, and Castriela doesn't find hers either. While attempting to "solve" the game (reconnect each person with their original name), we discover that many of us have not been able to relocate our original names and worse still, that some of our names no longer exist. These names, usually names that are unusual in this region or "difficult to pronounce" (a phrase often thrown back at people of color who ask to have their names spoken correctly), have been mangled and altered or even forgotten. Castriela's is one such name that is anglicized by clumsy ears, and no attempt is made to correct it, as whoever held her name in their mouth felt none of the significance of its loss. As a trans person, I also have a complex relationship with my name, and though my name is not destroyed as hers is, the fact that I never reclaim it still makes me uneasy.

This exercise, called Name Gumbo, is a common name game usually associated with Augusto Boal's Theater of the Oppressed. This example, from a workshop I attended in 2015, is just one of many ways my trans identity has left me alienated and frustrated in Applied Theater work. Of the innumerable theater workshops and classes I've attended, nearly all have begun with some form of a name game. All of these games are divorced from the complex relationship between trans identity and names, and thus I begin each new workshop already leaving a huge part of myself at the door. In these spaces, names are simply the first step in labeling and identifying one another so we can move on to more important work. Applied Theater is meant to bring people together, using tools of theater-making to help us build and connect and create change – but how can I do this work if I must ignore my transness to proceed? If I begin without a name, what could I possibly end with?

These questions served as the impetus behind my formation of the Transgressive Acts Trans Applied Theatre Troupe in the fall of 2014. As part of my MFA thesis work at the University of Massachusetts-Amherst, I developed and facilitated this troupe for three years, exploring Applied Theater through the lens of a trans-only space.

As a dramaturg, two of my primary goals are making sure a piece is accurate to and/or respectful of source material it draws upon and helping an audience understand and connect with that piece. As a trans dramaturg, I am often tasked with projects that have trans characters or subjects, and on these pieces I find myself asking if those two goals are mutually exclusive. In order to make plays that are intelligible to cisgender audiences (the primary demographic of most theaters), I (and the playwrights and directors I've worked with) often have to sacrifice accuracy and nuance of trans experience for the sake of clarity. I'm doing it right now as I write this chapter. I watch playwrights struggle with this conundrum daily, trying to put out work that will reach a broad audience while maintaining subjects that will not be readily accepted or even understood. Though the plays I work on are often by and about trans people, rarely are they for us. It is not enough that we play for cis people, but we must also play for ourselves.

As a genderqueer person, I perform a simplified version of my identity every day, allowing others to read me as simply a feminine man, ignoring the various pronouns and gendered labels thrown at me, and moving through the world with both the privileges of visible "maleness" and the oppressions of visible transness. I used to try harder to be understood as my true identity, but frankly it took far more emotional labor than I could muster on a daily basis, not to mention the dangers I encountered associated with constantly refuting the cisheteropatriarchy just by existing. It's a lot of work. Trans-only spaces have offered me a brief respite from this labor, and have been incredibly healing. After years of working in trans-only spaces in the non-profit sector, I wanted to apply this same framework to my theater practice. I was not disappointed. Having a space where I could be as messy, as illegible, and as full of gender paradoxes as I am, allowed me to also create work that was similarly nuanced and challenging.

Over the first two years of the troupe, I facilitated workshops in existing Applied Theater techniques, including Ping Chong's Undesirable Elements, Theater of the Oppressed, and Boal's more introspective work, Cops in the Head. In each workshop, I explored facilitating through a trans lens and asked my participants to reflect on the techniques' efficacy for them as trans theater-makers. Each time we clashed with the techniques, finding boundaries not built to hold the specific complexities of trans experiences. Within Undesirable Elements, the structure asks participants to create a linear narrative that links their stories to a metanarrative within the community. The winding, reversing, and complex ways trans people experience "coming of age" resisted this narrative, and our attempts to make it fit felt more like forcing our when our realities. Other techniques asked us to identify our "feminine nurturance" or "masculine postures" and other binary labels that foreclosed our creative fluidity. Some techniques, such as Boal's, asked us to accept our inner power and strength – but imagine asking a trans person whose very voice causes her dysphoria and trauma to think of said voice as her source of power. These tools were difficult and frequently painful.

I tried adapting the techniques to suit our needs, sometimes with more promising results, but we often found ourselves more frustrated than invigorated. It became clear to me that I needed to start designing new Applied Theater practices with trans people at the core. Just as the space needed to be designed for trans people, so did the techniques we used within it.

In the fall of 2016, I started bringing in new trans-specific activities, games, writing prompts, and devising work for the troupe to try. One thread emerged as key to much of this work: Names. Each of us had our own complex relationship with names, and each was specific to being both trans and our cultural/racial identities. Names can cause dysphoria, trigger memories of misgendering and being "clocked." They can build pride, as we choose our own new names or rebuild a relationship with a given name. Names can be a space of absence, when a new name lacks the history or familial connection usually a part of cisgender name narratives. But names can also be revolutionary, as gendered associations with names are stripped away, and our societal reliance on names is unpacked and dissolved. Thus was born the Trans Naming Workshop (TNW).

I developed the TNW as a set of Applied Theater exercises that asks trans participants to examine their relationship with their old name, work through associated traumas of dead-naming and misgendering, delve into the significance of names/name histories/linguistic and familial lineages, and finally perform a ritual in which they establish a new relationship with their chosen name. Since the first TNW, I have facilitated TNW with other trans groups, and I have tried to make the techniques freely available for other trans folks who wish to bring the TNW to their communities, so I won't detail each step here. I would like instead to skip to the end: the Naming Ritual.

The Fall of 2016 workshop and is now the last step of my TNW. The prompt for the Ritual contains only two questions, but what I learned in this very first TNW is what has fueled me to grow and develop this work.

Question One: What is asked of the trans person taking on the name?

When I brought this question in at first as a discussion topic, I felt fires break out in each of the six troupe members. At first it was a cacophony of angry comments about how trans people have to go through grueling legal processes for name changes or how universities and jobs rarely recognize chosen names without these legal changes. They condemned the amount of time and work and money that goes into a legal name change, when cis people call each other by nicknames all the time without batting an eyelash. A trans woman in the troupe who had chosen to retain her given name (a stereotypically masculine name) decried the swift pressure for newly out trans people to pick a new name, one more befitting their gender, even though some trans people wish not to change their name – or at least not so quickly. One participant who was not fully out complained about constantly reminding himself what his name was around this group or that group, and then having to remind everyone else what his name was too. A trans man in the troupe talked about the shame and disappointment he felt at his father not wanting him to take on the male family name because he could not live up to it. The conversation turned into bitterness at the ways trans people are forced to prove their names – or their gender, by way of their names. Always the discussion was about what was being asked of trans people by external forces, rather than what we are asking of ourselves. We were performing our names for others, never for us.

I used this discussion to fuel the first part of the Naming Ritual. I asked each participant to do research into their chosen names, their linguistic origins, others who have held the name, their etymology, and their familial history. We performed image theater of the names' meanings, then made tableaux depicting names' histories. We played with the stories of how each of us was given our old names and performed new stories for how we came to find these new names. Through this work, each participant was asked to find what their personal yardstick would be to measure whether they had fulfilled their name's call. I asked them to take my discussion question as a prompt to find a way to perform for themselves their connection to their name. One participant chose to focus on the etymology of his name, developing frozen images of himself depicting each of the traits the name was associated with. In his images, he became his name, proving only to himself that he already held its power. Another participant played with her name's visual beauty and lyrical sound, developing a brief dance that embodied its shape and melody.

Question Two: What is asked of the community in return?

As the participants worked independently with their names, I started to create a narrative for what would later become the Ritual. It is a call and response. It is a declaration and a witnessing. If the first step (the taking on of the names) is just for us, the second step is for our reconnection with the broader world. I asked the participants to think about what they would want from their communities when choosing a name. Do they want affirmation? Support? Defense? Help achieving their name's significance? Are they asking this of their religion? Their family? Which community? As I opened these questions to the troupe, participants' answers were much more hopeful than they had been in the prior discussion. Without the burden of the expected paths of legibility, they were able to envision the kinds of support and love and acceptance they would actually want to see. One word became hotly contested in this discussion: understanding. After one participant stated simply that she just wanted people to understand why she had chosen to keep her old name, another participant quickly retorted that he didn't care at all whether anyone understood him: he wanted them to respect his choice regardless. Another participant agreed, arguing that it would probably be impossible to achieve a real understanding without being trans themselves, but that love and support don't require understanding. I was reminded instantly of the labor I put into trying to produce trans theater that primarily cis audiences will connect to. Maybe this kind of trans theater, like an immersive study abroad program, could ask cis audiences to step entirely outside their realm of experience and just bear witness, knowing not all of it would "make sense."

From here, I asked participants what this "call and response" might look like performed. I asked them to take whatever result they were asking for from their community and turn it into something visible, tangible, or audible. I asked them to think about their call and response metaphorically, using their performance as a stand-in for an emotional response. The example I gave them ended up being part of my own Ritual later on. I told them in my call and response I would be asking my community to choose to either protect/defend my name and identity and/or to nourish me with love and affirmations. As an avid gardener, I used a flower pot as my metaphor. My community would be asked to add stones to the pot to protect the seedling or spoonfuls of water to nourish it. The use of metaphor as part of this narrative caught on, and soon each participant was building on their work from the previous step using metaphors that were connected to their own lives.

The results were stunning. Funny, vibrant, silly, emotional, deeply felt, and powerful. In late 2016, I asked each of the six participants to perform these Rituals for the troupe and a handful of guests they'd invited to witness.

One participant developed her piece from the dancing she'd done in the first part of the Ritual. She took the call and response to heart, developing choreographed movements that she taught us. We moved, and she moved back at us. She moved, and we moved back at her. The third time, somehow like a waltz, the movements came together – not identical, but connected.

One participant connected the idea of call and response to her heritage as a witch and the traditions of her spirituality. She traced the curves of her name into a sigil, imbued it with the power of her witch heritage, and asked us to burn it with her, such that each time her name would be written she would feel its significance.

One participant took what he'd learned about his name's etymology and wrote those words across his skin. "I will be heard" he wrote on one arm, asking then for us, as his witnesses, to come up and repeat the words back to him as we gently washed the marker from his skin, "You are heard, you are heard, you are heard."

Witnessing these moments of trans theater, I wonder what we could create if we did not have to worry who might understand us and instead ask simply to be heard. And it can start with names.

7   Translation and form

Julie Felise Dubiner

When I was in graduate school, I took a German translation class. It was a strange experience – we didn't learn to speak or pronounce the language, just to translate, and only from German into English. It was an intensive class, five days a week for four hours in class, plus hours of homework, for five weeks. And I loved it.

I loved my teacher. She was so powerful and smart. She had a languid Marlene Dietrich thing going on and was always all put together with that dark burgundy wine lipstick we loved in 1995, and she was seemingly completely unflappable. And she said something often in class which has stayed with me: Translation is an act of violence.

Translation is an act of violence

I think about that so much, not just from German to English, but from form to form, from page to stage. Yes, it is a dramatic statement, hyperbolic, maybe not even always true. But I'd like us to think about it more. I'd like us to think about accepting plays in their own place. Their own language. And their own structure. Too often we ask the creators to translate them, or we judge them for steadfastly remaining in their own language.

In school and in the literary life I chose (that chose me?) I learned a lot about structure. Similarly to how whiteness and maleness are centered as the norm in our American society, so I was taught to center Aristotelian structure as the form on which to judge all plays. Yes, I learned about other styles – but it was the comparative of Mayakovsky to O'Neill or Miller vs. Strindberg vs. Beckett. We read women from Hrosvita to Sor Juana and up through Hellman and Wellman and Wasserstein, but in my memory they were considered as "special," not normal – as were the embarrassingly few writers of color we read. I suppose this is what The Canon was in the 1980s or 90s according to the theater intelligentsia. I learned to evaluate plays in and of themselves, but it was always in relation to how they responded to Aristotelian markers – and Aristotelian markers of tragedy in particular.

Was that mental and literal translation an act of violence? I have come to believe it was and still is, with all the drama, hyperbole, and questionable truth inherent in the statement.

Question it with me. That is what I ask.

When I joined the American Revolutions project, it became my mission to find artists to commission that would represent diversity of form and style as well as diversity of ethnicity, race, religion, gender, and sexuality of the writers. It was tremendously freeing to read plays with that in mind. So much of the literary manager's life is spent reading for a specific artistic director. Some of those artistic directors are wonderful people who want to think expansively, but we still read to find plays that suit their tastes. I have spent so much of my career translating myself to someone else. This work felt good. It lacked violence.

This shift in my work coincided with a grand reckoning in the regional theaters, not to mention the United States and the world. I'll talk about theater and you can make of the microcosm as you want.

The regional theater movement that I inherited is one that doesn't naturally support work or artists that challenge a status quo that was set in stone sometime around the 1970s and 80s during the height of the subscriber heyday. Those days are over and aren't coming back, and I don't think we should miss them. We do need to come up with new producing models and better ways to take care of our artists and thrill our audiences, and maybe part of the key to these awaiting discoveries is to stop translating.

I am thinking now of so many playwrights and other creative artists my colleagues in literary offices and I have tried to champion, only to be told by even well-meaning artistic directors and season planning committees that they "didn't get it" or "it feels like it's not done." In the wake of the success of American Revolutions, I find myself dwelling on those comments and checking and re-checking myself to see if I challenged those remarks enough in the past. I don't think I did.

Have I gotten better at challenging them now?

I have.

Eventually there will be 37 plays from American Revolutions, all concerning moments of change in American history. In the time that I was

there, there was never a play that we brought to the season planning committee that was universally loved and approved. That's fine – I love to argue
about plays. But I kept hearing, keep hearing, even at OSF, where we there
is so much work being done around issues of equity, diversity, and inclusion, where there was at the time an artistic director who wanted to be an
expansive thinker, where new plays succeeded on any metric by which they
are measured, "I don't get it" or "It feels like it's not done."

I learned a powerful lesson when we produced *Party People* by Universes in 2012. There were concerns that the play wouldn't get "finished,"
and the artistic staff tried to step in and ask for changes in a way I knew
wasn't right. But I was new, it was the first play I was dramaturging at OSF,
and I did not follow my heart well enough. Universes, though, of course,
knew what they were doing and what they wanted, and I learned from them.
And I watched the audiences leap to their feet every performance and loved
that the show was loved in Berkeley and New York. Universes would not
allow themselves or their work to be translated.

When we were considering *Roe* by Lisa Loomer, the committee found
the play intriguing and exciting, but many weren't sure that the storytelling
was clear. As I listened to my very smart and very kind colleagues, I realized that Lisa's play was being met with that reaction because she hadn't
followed a traditional western storytelling structure. For those of us who
have been taught realism or naturalism or some half-remembered Aristotelian theories or Shakespeare as the proper form, the natural tendency was
to push back. But she was intentionally not using traditional form. She was
stretching the boundaries to tell a feminist story in a more feminist form.
We had to hold multiple thoughts in our heads at once; we had to like and
dislike the characters at the same time. We already knew the ending and
knew the ending could change. There was no one hero (or heroine), there
were two women holding equal weight and questioning each other and challenging the audience because both were simultaneously reliable and unreli-
able narrators of their own experience of recorded history. The agnorisis
and peripeteia repeated and morphed for both of them and were not in the
expected places. As we moved forward and into production, Lisa got so
many well-intentioned and good notes, and she took some of them, but she
stayed true to her form. She would not be translated. And again, the audiences loved the show loudly as it played out for them and leapt to their feet
at the end here and around the country.

I saw the same thing when we brought Karen Zacarias' hilarious and
brilliant *Destiny of Desire*. (Karen is an American Revolutions commissioned artist, but this is not her American Revolutions play.) It was treated

in consideration as "light" but was perhaps the most loved show of the 2018 OSF season, provoking passionate response to its story, style, and political commentary. Untranslated both in form and language. Brecht, telenovela, family drama, musical – all mixed together. Other shows have been harder for our audiences. Idris Goodwin's *The Way the Mountain Moved* also functioned off the grid of traditional narrative expectations. It is meant to be experienced as a hybrid of poetry and plot, combining and challenging the familiar cinematic form of the American Western, and for those able to let go and experience it, it is a remarkable piece of art and theater. And I am glad Idris wouldn't be translated.

One of the mistakes we institutional theater people have made in the past that hopefully we can correct as we lurch into the future is that we have asked plays to conform to a form even as we have tried to increase the diversity of art and artists we present on our stages. We have, often unintentionally, committed acts of violence against these writers and their work. We have not met them where they are and tried to learn their language. We have expected them to learn ours. We must do better at considering their stories as their stories and get better at taking magnificent leaps of faith with them as our audiences see and find themselves. We must stop judging a play for what it isn't and meet it as what it is. Stories are a way for people to share themselves and where they come from, what they have come to understand about the world that is to be shared through art. And it is our wonderful job to promote and share them.

These are the lessons I will take into the next season planning meetings I am at, the next conversation with an artistic director, or carry with me if I am the artistic director. To perform fewer acts of violence. And I can't wait to learn all these new languages.

Section Three

Who's "at the table"?

8 Crossing The Line

Jonathan Meth

Crossing The Line was a project of the partnership between Moomsteatern (Malmo, Sweden), Compagnie de l'Oiseau-Mouche (Roubaix, France), and Mind The Gap (Bradford, U.K.), three of Europe's leading theater companies making professional touring theater with learning-disabled artists. All three companies have been operating for more than thirty years. This was their first collaboration, and it came out of a joint conversation with me at the Accessing the Future of the Field event held by VSA (Very Special Arts) at the Kennedy Center in Washington DC, in September 2012. My case study will explore the intercultural diversity of learning-disabled performance dramaturgies in Crossing The Line.

The project, running from October 2014–January 2017, emerged two years after that first conversation. Crossing The Line initially featured learning-disabled artists from each of the three companies spending time at another one of the companies to observe and participate in their theater-making processes, as well as company staff learning about the other companies' structures, cultural systems, economic models, and strategic audience development activities. All of this culminated in a festival in Roubaix, which included performances by all three companies as well as films and industry debates.

As Project Dramaturg on Crossing The Line, my own role might best be described as curatorial. My presence within the project afforded me an opportunity to witness practices from all three companies and to explore the different cultural systems that had given rise to their work. I was also able to make and cement connections across the collaboration, building outwards to identify and engage with other artistically-led companies that make professional performance work with learning-disabled theater performers.

"While the idea of dramaturgy could imply a tendency towards systematization and management, at its best it implies responsiveness, an awareness of the connections between things and is able to both facilitate and critique them," offer critics Turner and Behrndt.[1] My dramaturgical involvement began from the project's inception, as I coordinated the project's EU funding bid via a process of assemblage. This was constructed around a discourse between partners based on a rolling system of offers and requests. In this chapter I will move back and forth between the opening session of the Crossing The Line project held in Bradford (see Figure 8.1) and the closing festival held in Roubaix nearly two years later. This moving back and forth is a deliberate dramaturgical strategy, as the terrain is as yet neither well-marked nor uncontested. My discussion will include reflections upon the practical theater-making processes I experienced, such as workshops, rehearsals, productions, and the Roubaix Festival, as well as issues pertinent to the wider cultural contexts in which the work was made. I will also draw on theoretical frameworks provided thus far within theater and learning disability and in particular from Matt Hargrave's *Theaters of Learning Disability – Good, Bad or Plain Ugly?*[2] This was the first book to explore the aesthetics of learning-disabled performance – as distinct from a focus on therapy or advocacy – and as project dramaturg it was the key text that accompanied me on my Crossing The Line journey.

One of the challenges of engagement with work made by learning-disabled artists (which may also include artists who identify as autistic) is the number of paradoxes, or at least unfixed and therefore unstable issues, it throws up. For example, the combining of "disabled" and "diverse" (in this case neurodiverse) as terms for performers who may identify as autistic is akin to the term "D/deaf" as delineating a separation between definitions that acknowledge deafness as a disability and those that assert it rather as a different way of being in the world – one that gives primacy to Sign Language.[3] As with the D/deaf model, the autistic self-advocacy movement contests the normative trope via a clear resistance to any medicalized notions of cure.[4]

How then to articulate and navigate these shifting positions? In his chapter on the work of Mind The Gap, Dave Calvert establishes a distinction between performance work made by physically or sensorially disabled performers and those who are learning-disabled:[5]

> The political impact of learning-disabled performance is no longer restricted to Graeae's early observance of disability rights, redressing a power imbalance and educating non-disabled audiences. By exposing performance conventions as limited and frustrating, actors with learning disabilities produce and demand the restless redefinition of theatrical – and by extension social – possibilities.[6]

More recently still, self-advocacy pioneers of neurodiversity, such as Jon Adams of Flow Observatorium, have sought to distinguish the term "disabled" from, for example, "autistic."

> The neurodiversity movement has led to a shift in approach as researchers concede to a growing and increasingly powerful distinctive discourse of autism rights, social justice, and refections on the creative aspects of autism.[7]

Frontiers

There's a frontier or border you have to cross to work transnationally. Euphemistically, if you're crossing a line, you're doing something a bit naughty, a bit forbidden – and if you're working with learning-disabled artists, you're frequently doing that in terms of any so-called mainstream aesthetic. "Crossing The Line" as a term gives a nod to shot rhetoric in the film world.[8] Cinematographic convention suggests that two characters in a scene should maintain the same left/right relationship to one another in the frame. If you want to disrupt the spectator's understanding of what they're seeing, then you cross that 180-degree line.

In the socializing area in the Mind The Gap building in Bradford, the TV plays images from the guest companies' productions so that as they arrive the companies' participants can see themselves and their colleagues. Mind The Gap (MTG) Resident Director Joyce Nga Yu Lee introduces the opening session in Bradford by stating that in Hong Kong a teacher described theater as a collaborative risk in action. It is in this spirit that she launches the first Crossing The Line workshop. Lee approaches the difficulties of translation with a creative flourish, jumping over the issue of comprehensibility by running the session in Cantonese – among those present, a language that only she understands. This is of course combined with visual clues. The creative challenges of access for learning-disabled artists, as well as those of translation, are immediately connected in our minds. Each requires a practical, dramaturgical strategy. By equalizing all participants' access with this choice of Cantonese, the session works very effectively.

Lee then deploys Tim Wheeler's[9] "Two By Three By Bradford" version of an Augusto Boal game. In pairs, participants begin counting: one, two, three – each partner says one number at a time. Once this has been mastered, the count number one is replaced with a sound. Then count number two is replaced with a physical action. Then count number three is replaced with a sound and a physical action. Then the exercise is re-run with the whole group standing in a circle. The artists engage with permission to be seen, gestures, and moving images. Stories emerge, but their narrative is created in the minds of those watching from the side (the audience).

In the next day's session, Mind The Gap Guest Director Alan Lyddiard draws on Boal but also on Kantor and his own wealth of experience as theater director and community theater-maker to welcome participants into a workshop that will feed the Contained Development process.[10] "I want to be like somebody else once was" is the opening line of Peter Hand-ke's *Kaspar*.[11] The play depicts a near-speechless young man destroyed by society's attempts to impose on him its language and its own "ratio-nal" values.[12] In the Bradford rehearsal workshop the line is also deployed in French – "Je veux etre quelqu'un d'autre qui a été." This sentence is adopted by Lyddiard and becomes an individual and collective rhythmic chant. As a dramaturgical signifier for theater-making, the process delib-erately selects and then rejects what is widely understood as a play (text) and repurposes the opening line away from its readily yielded meaning to become a tool for another kind of theater (and meaning)-making: one that might combine sounds or textures of individual and collective Swedish, French, English. . . .

Lyddiard's slow walking builds layers through physical, simple move-ment sequencing. Daily morning warm-up exercises are given, as Lyddi-ard articulates it, "authentically – completely – sincerely" (all slippery words, to use Hargrave's phrase, in any language). There is rooting/rout-ing the performers to/through the space, each other, and themselves, and live music runs alongside. Jez Colborne (Mind The Gap resident artist) extemporizes on the keyboard. This serves to anchor, steer, and under-score. Individual, personal stories begin to emerge from the participants, with Lyddiard refining what works and what doesn't. Next, Lyddiard adds technology: screens, microphones, and video cameras. These allow the generation of snippets: slow walking, stories to microphone, the moving of the screen and cables – three things going on at the same time. Starting with the personal stories, the action picks up pace, with the performers developing awareness of others in the space, as yet seemingly in a random order. Lyddiard watches, assesses, then creates further instructions that focus on the newly emerging performance text: timing, refining, pick-ing up the process again. There is room for a different original creative contribution, this time in French, from Compagnie de l'Oiseau-Mouche performer Thierry Dupont. Simply stated emotions work with the mate-rial that is generated: the build is iterative, recursive. Lyddiard's session concludes with the entire sequence run, so everyone has a sense of what has been attempted and accomplished.

Hargrave introduces the notion of dis-precision, which can be understood as a disruption that allows an extra dimension in perspective: "little tear marks in the performance where the audience is able to see the joins created in rehearsal: the blocking that's been learned through repetition. 'Seeing the join,' a continuous deconstruction between the performer and the text . . ."[13] Here Hargrave is positing the need for a reconsideration of the actor's craft, away from a more conventionally understood conservatoire training in relationship to how an audience might engage with such a performance. Lyddiard makes the distinction between "actor" and "performer," preferring the latter as a term to describe a process of the people onstage self-presenting. With the very personal snippets of performers' stories created through this process of assemblage, the effect of the final production on the spectators shifts between Brechtian presentation to the post-dramatic. The title "Contained" rather elegantly illustrates the paradox here, as a consistent reading won't hold.

The Mind The Gap (MTG) Ambassadors, drawn from the company, have been working throughout the four days, welcoming, hosting, explaining, and asking questions of visitors. In their final session, they use MTGTV recording as a tool both for creative engagement with the guests and for developing specific skills to allow for reflection on what has been the participants' experiences.

What happens to territory if the center is everywhere?

The Mind The Gap decision to combine this opening artist residency with an industry-facing day-long symposium (March 2015) allowed the work to be linked to its cultural context(s): raising questions, providing challenges, and opening up the process and the discourse to the three companies and around eighty industry professionals and academics.

The history of U.K. performance in regard to physically and/or sensorially-disabled artists is not congruent with the history of their learning-disabled counterparts. They may share similar values, but the discourse(s) in the U.K. around the former can tend to occlude the latter. Hargrave identifies learning disability as "an unstable category that stands for a range of complex social processes." He defines the subject of his book as "theater involving the collaboration of learning-disabled artists, which articulates a process rather than a fixed point."[14]

In the workshop the day before, performer/musician and Mind The Gap resident artist Jez Colborne told me that sirens are "different": differently powered. Some work with engines; some are powered by air. Each country might choose the one they think most powerful, but they all have varying pitch and tone. (Colborne is something of an expert on sirens, and his fascination with them led to the 2012 Mind The Gap show *Irresistible*, described as a siren symphony.)

"Perhaps universal history is the history of the various intonations of a few metaphors," Borges concludes in his 1951 essay/note, "Pascal's Sphere."[15] Taking as its central tenet the premise, "God is an intelligible sphere, whose centre is everywhere, and whose circumference is nowhere," Borges' text takes us, in three pages, through the history of this idea from Xenophanes via Parmenides to twelfth-century poet and theologian Alain of Lille. This is in turn adapted by Pascal to "Nature is an infinite sphere, the centre of which is everywhere, the circumference nowhere," which is itself in turn amended by the critical edition of *Tourneur* (Paris, 1941), of which the Brunschvieg edition reproduces the cancellations and hesitations in the manuscript, revealing that Pascal started to write the word "effroyable": "a frightful sphere, the centre of which is everywhere, and the circumference nowhere." While persistent, the spherical metaphor is both iterative and unstable.

In this context, the construct of Mainstream and Margins as a framework with which to consider diversity can be called into question. What if, *pace* Borges, the center is everywhere? I argue that the task then becomes curatorial from wherever your center happens to be. This might require divergent as well as convergent thinking; that as learning-disabled artists, we are shapeshifters with multivalent identities. If, in Dave Calvert's words at the Bradford symposium, "culture can take a different path to articulating and exploring who we are and who we want to be,"[16] might it be helpful to think of learning-disabled theater as a kind of Schrödinger's theater[17] – that is, simultaneously disabled and not disabled?

Fixing territory in place – as might reasonably be sought by those of an activist inclination – should only be the focus if (counter-)colonization is the goal. Otherwise the challenge becomes to investigate and embrace de-territorialized attributes and behaviors. In this way the aesthetics and the politics are entwined. The structural model of the institutional monolith may no longer be conventionally workable. For example, the Royal Opera House opening its doors to showcase the homeless (*With One Voice* was a festival in 2012 that saw three hundred people who had experienced homelessness perform at Covent Garden) is still operating as a form of *noblesse oblige*, as it is fundamentally a top-down structure. Territory may be more productively defined by its constituent parts, which is why partnerships are key. Rather than aspiring to the mainstream monolith, fluidity, mobility, and engagement in a more constellatory landscape represent an important shift. De Certeau is useful here in *The Practice of Everyday Life* when he states, "Everyday life invents itself by poaching in countless ways on the property of others."[18] He advocates for moving away from "imposed systems," a creation of "a space for manoeuvres of unequal forces and for utopian points of reference."[19]

What constitutes value?

One of the focal points of the symposium was the quality of – and the discourse around – the work. Within the context of "unequal forces and utopian points of reference," who values what and how? What is the permission or the benediction being sought? How do we define what constitutes peer review? Aesthetics and politics – are they productively separable? *Guardian* theater critic Lyn Gardner made an analogy with children's theater in the U.K., which had seemed somewhat straitjacketed by several factors. Preeminent was the economic issue of children and their relationship to theater being largely mediated in the U.K. via formal education settings that impact the aesthetic parameters of the work. First, Gardner asserted, those making work had to disentangle themselves from the perceived Theater-in-Education/Youth Theater/Theater for Young People morass.

Purni Morell's diverse international perspectives allowed her to cut through any such morass when she took up her post at Unicorn Theatre. "It is this refusal to separate children's issues and national issues – to view children as in any way distinct from the 'bigger picture' – that is helping Morell transform the Unicorn into one of the most passionate and relevant theatres in Britain today," says Miriam Gillinson in an interview with her.[20] In a similar vein, wrestling with any static sense of an aesthetics and politics dynamic is essential to the growth of learning-disabled performance work. Moreover, intercultural collaboration is the ideal territory/non-territory to explore aesthetics and politics because it allows for different ways of working across different countries and languages to emerge alongside each other and see where any cross-pollination might lead.

Hargrave asserted in the symposium that conversations about quality are about redistribution of power.[21] The hierarchies of theater reviewing need to be laid bare:[22] newspaper editor, arts editor, first string (commercial), second string. Who is writing/talking about what to whom? What is perceived to be at stake by whom? How is the changed landscape of bloggers, embedded criticism, and academics altering the possibilities of discourse? To what extent does the blogosphere overturn these hierarchies? When chairing a debate on disability aesthetics in Roubaix as part of the culminating

Crossing The Line Festival, I was rightly checked by freelance journalist Bella Todd when I asserted that we lack a theater criticism commensurate with the aesthetics and politics of learning-disabled theater-making. Todd had been supported to cover the Crossing The Line Festival by the British Council. In the absence of mainstream U.K. press at the event (although this was not the case with their French counterparts), Todd reminded us that there are freelance journalists writing with a nuanced acculturation to some of the aesthetic, political, and economic challenges facing professional, touring, learning-disabled theater work. It all depends on where you look and on being willing to take different parts of the theater industry on a journey with you.

Theater viewed merely as commodity trades on the imprimatur of key gatekeepers: critics, policy-makers, and funders; trusted industry peers. At the Bradford symposium Hargrave asked how a work's guiding intention can achieve an aesthetic that then transmits to an external audience.[23] Or, in other words, how do all these paradoxes go to market? Of course, they do not go in a straight line, but if we take allies on a journey (bringing along venues, festivals, programmers, and marketing departments, as well as critics and academics) we have to be clear about the stages of that journey – and so do they. Ben Evans, Head of Arts and Disability, EU Region, at the British Council, said in Bradford that he could not have a conversation about disability theater with continental colleagues. Rather, he must pitch it as part of "the best ten pieces of work" coming out of the U.K.[24] Does this collapse or constrain the whole debate around quality, particularly when viewed through the lens suggested by Calvert's assertion at the beginning of this chapter?

Yet the three companies involved have all been making learning disabled theater for more than thirty years. They're arguably at the top of their game. Crossing The Line is the first international collaboration involving this heightened level of expertise and scope – together with the extent of differences in approach. Typically, festivals have a single programmer curating around a particular thematic focus. The Crossing The Line festival grew out of a twenty-seven-month project. The culminating festival was not just about the shows but about understanding how they have come about: from workshops giving insight into the processes, to roundtables that go into wider contextual issues around European collaborative working and disability aesthetics. The Crossing The Line festival was an opportunity for the different teams of artists to spend time getting to meet their peers, see the work, scrutinize the work – to challenge themselves, calibrate themselves, celebrate themselves.

Two years on from the first Crossing The Line Bradford symposium, with the culmination of the Crossing The Line project and the festival of all three companies' work in Roubaix, Evans would go on to describe the work of learning-disabled artists as

> the last avant-garde movement. I was very struck by the deep under-standing that the project partners had of each other's work, compa-nies and aims. They each have distinct aims and local conditions, and yet there was a rare knowledge of, and sensitivity to, the work of the other companies. To me the festival definitely did not feel competitive – but rather displayed a genuine curiosity about each other's practice. This feels like a wonderfully European event. Three key companies with many years of experience, learning more about themselves and their practice through collaboration and comparison – the international mutuality strengthening all partners.[25]

Complex ecology

An important aspect of the Crossing The Line companies' journeys has been to connect with how other countries negotiate their own systems and struc-tures through different historical-political, economic, and aesthetic lenses. France structures its arts provision in such a way that it likes to have one of everything that signifies excellence. This is Compagnie de l'Oiseau Mouche: the best when it comes to learning-disabled theater. Because of that, the com-pany has been able to jump over a lot of debates that the U.K. has been having about "disability arts" versus "artists with a disability." According to Stephane Frimat, Compagnie de l'Oiseau-Mouche's Artistic Director, when they propose a latest work to the French touring circuit, it's largely down to taste, economics, and logistics, rather than disability per se, as to whether or not it gets programmed.[26] In their view, "nous sommes tous Francais" – and so "neuro-diverse," for example, is not such a nominated focus. In France, because of the way that country structures its arts provision and cultural offerings, Compagnie de l'Oiseau Mouche has developed via a differ-ent trajectory than, for instance, Mind The Gap in the U.K. As a regional, national, and increasingly international touring company, viewed as a center of excellence, with a wide variety of artistic input from a broad range of guest directors working under the overall curation of Stephane Frimat and his team, Compagnie de l'Oiseau-Mouche operates in the same milieu as any French touring theater company, with access to the national agencies, such as ONDA (the French Office for Contemporary Arts circulation), and their sup-port. In this sense, the metaphorical center-is-everywhere cultural policy of national centers has allowed Compagnie de l'Oiseau-Mouche to effectively circumvent the British model of Disability Arts.

Broadly, the Compagnie de l'Oiseau-Mouche approach is to train audiences. Its approach is to develop critical judgement, across broader social strata, through a process of acculturation. Different audiences are identified, such as "marginalized groups," family, the elderly, learners, citizen participants. The question the company asks is: how can Compagnie de l'Oiseau-Mouche build lasting relationships with audiences, rather than put bums on seats? The reality of Roubaix (a working class, culturally mixed Northern French town on the outskirts of its richer neighbor, Lille – a relationship not unlike that between Bradford and Leeds in the U.K.) is "how do I fill the fridge?" rather than "what is the next show I will come to?" The impetus, then, is to make the theater open to the outside: challenging prejudices and expectations about theater. So it might be "come to a show" but also "come to the building, a workshop, a rehearsal." Connecting the ensemble to the public is part of the process. Note – there is no mention of disability in this discourse whatsoever.

The fact the Compagnie de l'Oiseau-Mouche team didn't take part in the informal roundtable on disability aesthetics at the culminating Festival

Figure 8.1 Left to right, Myriam Baïche, Valérie Waroquier, Thierry Dupont, and Joyce Nga Yu Lee

Source: Photography credit Jonathan Meth

in Roubaix – although there were associates in the audience who contributed substantively to the discussion – illustrates the paradoxical nature of the curatorial task. Formally, in France they just don't "go there" in that way. In the U.K., there has been a forty-plus year battle to get to the point where disabled practitioners can demand to be artistically engaged with and artistically driven. The U.K. also operates a mixed economy. Practitioners are obliged to be creative in how they access resources: you combine training, education, and learning with employment, and then you find routes to money however you can.

In Sweden, Moomsteatern's director Per Törnqvist made the decision to declare "we are a theater company, we make theater" and to reject the dominant funding streams – and the strings that come with it – from social services, education, or health. At a national level, they are understood as a Swedish cultural asset because they don't go the "social" route. But a certain amount of chutzpah is also involved. When they worked with Slovenian partners, Moomsteatern found a way of commandeering the Swedish military air force into flying them there, by discovering a loophole in Swedish law that obliged the air force to accommodate them. In all these structures and differing systems, there have to be charismatic, canny, resourceful, and visionary individuals to really make a change.

In this way, Moomsteatern had to take on – and change – the law in order to create a permanent, employed ensemble company of seven learning-disabled theater makers. Nevertheless, even when formally eschewing funding from a social route – and indeed to varying degrees this is the case across all three Crossing The Line companies – the curatorial practice around learning-disabled theater-making involves gatekeeping across education, social services, housing, and employment sections of society. So, the companies are resolutely artistically led but curating a much more complex ecology, as it were, beneath the waterline.

Inhabiting the paradoxes

I want to return to the notion of Schrödinger's theater – one in which the audience is asked to both consider and disregard the "disabled" in the "disabled performer." Kuppers sets up a stark paradox, which the disabled artist either implicitly or explicitly inhabits.[27]

> The disabled performer is marginalised and invisible – relegated to borderlands far outside the central area of cultural activity, into the discourses of medicine, therapy and victimhood. At the same time people with physical impairments are also hypervisible, instantly defined in

their physicality. The physically impaired performer has therefore to negotiate two areas of cultural meaning: invisibility as an active member of the public sphere, and hypervisibility and instant categorization.

Stuart Hall's response to Salman Rushdie as part of an exchange of correspondence following the release of Black Audio Film Collective's *Handsworth's Songs*, directed by John Akomfrah, maps out some of the problematics of the terrain and how easy it can be to misstep. The very absence of disability from this particular discourse – which posits an explicit intersection between gender, race, ethnicity, sexuality, and class – leaves us a space in which to consider disability aesthetics and the politics thereof.

> Once you enter the politics of the end of the essential black subject you are plunged headlong into the maelstrom of a continuously contingent, unguaranteed, political argument and debate: a critical politics, a politics of criticism. You can no longer conduct black politics through the strategy of a simple set of reversals, putting in the place of the bad old essential white subject, the new essentially good black subject.[28]

In citing both Kuppers and Hall, I am arguing for the need to occupy a space within the paradox.

There's a really interesting relationship between the dramaturgy of translation and how work can be made accessible within a learning-disabled performance context. I would argue that as a non-Swedish speaker you have to surrender to a piece like Moomsteatern's version of Strindberg's *A Dream Play* in the original Swedish, which they brought to the Crossing The Line festival in Roubaix. What happens when you go to watch a piece of theater in a language you fundamentally don't understand? First of all, there's a struggle to use the bit of your mind you usually use. Then you go through phases of discomfort, frustration, boredom. Then you either zone out or something more challenging happens: the customary way you watch shuts down and creates a space for something else to happen. This is, for me, analogous to watching performances made by learning-disabled theater makers. You have to access the work differently. You have to access yourself differently.

Notes

1 Cathy Turner and Synne Behrndt, *Dramaturgy and Performance* (Basingstoke: Palgrave Macmillan, 2008), 37.
2 Matt Hargrave, *Theatres of Learning Disability – Good, Bad or Plain Ugly?* (London: Palgrave Macmillan, 2015).

3 In 1972, Professor James Woodward, co-director of the Centre for Sign Linguistics and Deaf Studies at the Chinese University of Hong Kong since 2004, proposed a distinction between deafness and the Deaf culture. He suggested using *deaf* (written with a lower case *d*) to refer to the audiological condition of deafness, and *Deaf* (written with an upper case *D*) to refer to Deaf culture. Carol A. Padden and Tom Humphries, *Inside Deaf Culture* (Cambridge, MA: Harvard University Press, 2005), 1.

4 Those proposing the medical model of disability identify mental differences as "disorders, deficits, and dysfunctions." From this point of view, some neurominority states are treated as medical conditions that can and should be corrected. David Pollak sees neurodiversity as an inclusive term that refers to the equality of all possible mental states. Available online at www.disabled-world.com/disability/awareness/neurodiversity/.

5 Here I use an adjectival formulation to underline the social as opposed to medical model of disability. People are disabled by society's inability to make adequate necessary adjustment to meet an individual's needs, thus creating a disabling world, as opposed to a medicalized model that focuses on pathology, e.g. people with disabilities (noun). This is not to entirely disavow the latter in favor of the former.

6 Dave Calvert, "Mind the Gap," 127–153, in *British Theatre Companies 1995–2014* (London: Bloomsbury Methuen, 2015), 150.

7 Bonnie Evans, *The Metamorphosis of Autism* (Manchester: Manchester University Press, 2017), 417.

8 Nicholas T. Proferes, *Film Directing Fundamentals* (Amsterdam: Focal Press, 2005), 5–7.

9 Tim Wheeler was the co-founder of Mind The Gap and its Artistic Director from 1988–2014.

10 Billed as "True Stories for The Heart," *Contained* was described by Mind The Gap in their promotional material as "a circle of projects, which surround a piece of high-quality theatre. Each element – including a music video, a series of short films, an exhibition – feed off each other artistically building long lasting relationships with people locally, nationally and internationally: more than just a performance; *Contained* is a concept, the start of a conversation."

11 Peter Handke, *Kaspar Hause* (London: Methuen, 1972).

12 Per Törnqvist, Artistic Director of Moomsteatern, explained in the session on text and script adaptation held in Malmo, that Moomsteatern were planning a new show – with no non-disabled freelancers – which would be an experiment for a six-plus age group audience: an adaptation of *Kaspar Hause*. Seven actors, seven scenes: so each actor would take responsibility for one key scene. This method, Törnqvist explained, aims to widen the responsibility and foster independence.

13 Hargrave, Matt (2009), 'Pure products go Crazy' Research in Drama Education 14:1, pp. 37–54 (Cited in Calvert, 2015, p. 150).

14 Ibid., 21–44.

15 Jorge Luis Borges, "Pascal's Sphere," in *Other Inquisitions, 1937–1952* (Austin, TX: University of Texas Press, 1993), 205.

16 Dave Calvert, in conversation at the Bradford symposium, March 15, 2014.

17 Schrödinger's cat is a thought experiment, sometimes described as a paradox, devised by Austrian physicist Erwin Schrödinger in 1935. It illustrates what he

saw as the problem of the Copenhagen interpretation of quantum mechanics applied to everyday objects. The scenario presents a cat that may be simultaneously both alive and dead.

18 Michel De Certeau, *The Practice of Everyday Life* (Berkeley, CA: University of California Press, 1980) translated from the French by Stephen Rendall, 2011, "Introduction," xi.

19 Ibid., 18.

20 Miriam Gillinson's interview with outgoing Unicorn Theatre Artistic Director Purni Morell, available online at http://exeuntmagazine.com/features/childs-play/.

21 Matt Hargrave, in conversation at the Bradford symposium, March 15, 2014.

22 It was announced at this time, in May 2018, that after 23 years Lyn Gardner would not have her contract renewed by the *Guardian*.

23 Matt Hargrave, in conversation at the Bradford symposium, March 15, 2014.

24 Ben Evans, Head of Arts and Disability, EU Region, British Council, in conversation at the Bradford symposium, March 15, 2014.

25 Ben Evans, in written feedback to the January 2017 Crossing The Line Festival in Roubaix.

26 Stephane Frimat, in conversation during the January 2017 Crossing The Line Festival in Roubaix.

27 Petra Kuppers, "Deconstructing Images Performing Disability," 25–40 in *Contemporary Theatre Review*, 3–4 (2001).

28 Stuart Hall's response to Salman Rushdie as part of an exchange of correspondence following the release of Black Audio Film Collective's *Handsworth's Songs*, directed by John Akomfrah, available online at www.diagonalthoughts.com/?p=134.

9 *Depth Perception*

Re-thinking social roles, staging Asperger's from the inside

Tim Collingwood

The idea for writing a play about my experiences with Asperger's came after I had decided to own my ability status and to take pride in something that, socially, people aren't taught to take pride in. From early adolescence, I had found solace in theater because it was a place where I didn't feel weird and could express myself productively as a member of society. I originally considered writing a play about Asperger's in high school, but I didn't have the confidence to go through with it. I was learning to be my own advocate, and theater was indirectly teaching me about cues and scripts but mostly about how to live in the world with confidence. It wasn't till after I'd finished college that I felt self-assured enough to sit down and write a play about the realities of Asperger's in my world.

The idea for my play, *Depth Perception*, came out of a desire to challenge the narrative of disability on stage through a theatrical rendering of the experiences that had led me to own my disability. I originally wrote a 50-page play about the transition from living with Asperger's – a path that had taken me from feelings of shame about my "condition" to an active experience of agency and the capacity to confront and resist negative societal reinforcements. Through therapy in college, I spent three years dissecting the labels I lived with, the judgments of others, and the internalized ableism that prevailed around me. Such labels and judgments had made it hard for me to own this part of myself and to make peace with my experiences. When we look into the mirrors offered by others, it is all too easy to see an other-abled self in terms of "dis"-words: "dis"ability, "dis"tortion, "dis"interest. In *Depth Perception* I wanted to capture the joy and the agency of "otherness," to capture myself as a unique human being. I wanted to capture also a transition that society doesn't encourage for people of different neurologies (under which I "qualified"). I spent hours writing and many hours revising and editing as well, because plays are never done.

My first production task was to get a director and actors – all I had so far was an idea and a script. I first sought a director among my friends, but they had their own projects, and nobody signed up. I then went to the performing arts listing network, stating that I needed a director for *Depth Perception* and that I wanted to email and talk with anyone who might be interested. I received a couple of emails and arranged a few phone calls. Due to the sensitive nature of the play, I wanted a director who could work with my singular experience of Asperger's: this wasn't going to be a "typical" disability play where the able-bodied/able-minded protagonist tested his skills via encounters/dramatic arcs with a disabled supporting character, nor was it to be a play in which a director gave an able-bodied protagonist instructions as to how to "play" Asperger's. I needed a director who would make artistic choices that could challenge conventional ideas of the relationship between lived experience and representation. I ended up finding a director who was also a colleague – someone who really wanted to help embody my vision.

Now the next challenge: actors. I went to the performing arts listing to find actors and said more about the play, asking for contact from anyone interested in acting. To a degree I was able to pull from actors I already knew, but I needed an actor to play the best-friend character who journeys from "ignorant child" to the role of "understood friend." I was able to find an actor and was excited to find that this actor also had Asperger's and was intrigued by the idea of a play that challenged conventional narratives. It felt good to work with a peer-in-struggle in an ableist society. I found myself deeply valuing their insights into the script, and I was constantly asking them – to the point of almost usurping my role as actor/ playwright – whether or not the script felt true to them, too. Of course, the rest of the cast's feedback was valuable, but I am not going to discredit the special influence of this particular peer because I was afraid of falling into the trap of creating a generalization about Asperger's and a universal experience about what it is and means for everybody who is medically/ socially defined by it. Such defining universals would, I felt, be counterproductive to the play's scope and specificity. I only wanted to speak about my experiences with it, and, by so doing, to represent on stage the uniqueness of a human being who is often labelled and obscured by the markers of "a condition." In the very act of seeking to assist a person with Asperger's, such labels can actually be the tools of alienation, rendering us aliens in a world that doesn't accept Asperger's for the human condition – challenging, frustrating, beautiful – that it is. The drama of the play concerns someone with a difference trying to survive in a world that doesn't make non-medicalized room for this difference: a person who is able, eventually, to celebrate their humanity in the process of rebuking such labels.

Rehearsals were spotty, and from time to time my director couldn't attend. This did not create conflict with the theater that produced the work, but it was difficult for me. I was an actor in my play, but suddenly I was "acting" as director for a day with no training at all, trying to play my scripted part while sending the director notes from my new, forcibly adopted role as part-time director. As a self-identified "Aspie," it is particularly difficult to disrupt or bifurcate my focus. Sometimes my work as producer (as well as intermittent director) got in the way of my getting off-book, not to mention that the "book" kept changing because we were hearing the lines differently in rehearsal and frequently needing to change them. I worked very hard at not being a playwright who was trying to act as well; I tried to separate myself from my own work so that I could memorize my lines. Eventually I did memorize them and the show did go on.

The way I wrote the script was purposefully non-linear, because I wanted to show the way in which "normal" psychology attempts to delineate Asperger's, to wrestle it to the ground and find a static pigeonhole for it. There would be flashbacks to childhood and adolescence – for example, there was a scene where I was playing baseball with a childhood friend who got annoyed with what he saw as my level of fixation on the sport. I felt hurt by his words and by his labelling of "fascination" as "fixation." There was a scene from my adolescence where my impassioned commentary about George W. Bush and the Dixie Chicks and political injustice provoked my childhood friend to wearily advise me that I didn't need to stress my points so much. I wanted to show on-stage how I internalized that as a judgment, with the "positive" engendering its own weirdly negative counterpart. Between the scenes, there would be a therapist character who offered perspective and reminded my character of how all of this was within the range of "normal," while my character responded – through the forcible internalization of ableism – by saying how *not* normal it was. Why try to placate me by using words like "normal"? "Normal" had never been my forte.

The play we performed was a fifteen-minute exploration of a developing work, but it covered a lot of ground, as the chosen excerpt was the beginning of the full work I envisioned. It covered briefly trying to fit in at college through consumption of alcohol and dancing drunk to a Stevie Nicks song, all the while dissecting my past to explain my theatrical present, with my character attempting to present a theatrical argument about the normalcy of Asperger's. I wanted to suggest, as my character came fully to embody his Asperger's, that "normal" is a condition that needs to be expanded (or even perhaps expended).

The feedback I got was varied. Because of Cleveland Public Theatre's open policy toward sharing new work, I attended every talkback and read every commentary card. The comments I remember getting suggested that people did want to see more; that I captured Asperger's perfectly on stage; and that there were things worth exploring from that fifteen-minute sample. The main negative criticism I got was that I should be wary not to share too personal a story on-stage (what is "fact" and what is theatrical "truth"?) and that maybe someone else should have played this version of me so as to give a measure of distance. I can understand that need, but I didn't want a neurotypical actor to portray me because that would bring in the Method approach, requiring the actor to spend time observing me to "get their role right." In other words, this approach would alienate me further from the neurotypical standards of normalcy, and it wouldn't expand "normal" at all. I didn't want to be made into a Forrest Gump, a Rain Man, or a Charlie Gordon from *Flowers for Algernon*: I just wanted myself to be seen for all the nuances and complexities in which my Asperger's plays a part. It's plausible to imagine that if I let someone with Asperger's or autism portray me, it would be helpful for future productions: but they have their own story to tell, and it's not mine, and at that time I was possessive of my own journey. I felt honored to have had (and created) this opportunity and was determined to use all comments constructively.

I think that to change the narrative of any marginalized group involves not only supporting the voices of the marginalized in theater through production and opportunity, but also asking questions about approaches to exploration and challenging received assumptions through that production. For *Depth Perception*, the title alone created a pause because it spoke to the reality of the Aspie experience, and it put the onus on the viewer (the perceiver) to delve more fully into the depths of my character. It centered my Aspie voice. In this production, the questions I had in the moment had little to do with questioning how my authenticity was expressed on stage and a great deal to do with how to express my truth theatrically. I wanted to change the way people think about intactness and un-intactness, ability and disability, in terms of a "condition" whose label isn't often challenged in society even though it is more and more extensively researched. And the questions that emerged were so important. If this play were to be fully written and produced in a full-length capacity, how would the flashbacks be seen? There were no light changes in the excerpt we produced because of the capture of real time; but would changing the lighting for those flashback scenes add to the abstraction of Asperger's, further distancing it from an ableist society? Or would it permit me to use ableist modes to illuminate my world, turning the tables on a society that has conventionally used my wayward condition to consolidate ideas about normalcy? Should actors of different neurologies be cast in the play and, if so, how would that impact the script and the production process? Should there be a balance of ableist-bodied/ableist-minded actors with actors of different neurologies and abilities? These are questions I am still asking myself, and when I return to the script to read it over and possibly update it, I want to push these questions and see how they might bridge the gap between the stage and the seats, between ableism and other ways of being.

Figure 9.1 Tim Collingwood, 2019

Source: Photography credit Sebastian H. Orr

10 Decolonizing "equity, diversity, and inclusion"

Strategies for resisting white supremacy

Annalisa Dias

Before beginning: a pause, positioning myself as speaker

As part of a podcast, I was recently asked to talk about my journey into the work of decolonization in theater practice. I joked that my ancestors colonized my other ancestors, so I carry deeply in my blood and bones the legacy of both colonizer and colonized. My father is from Goa (a former Portuguese colony that is part of what is now called India), and my mother's ancestry is mostly Western European. My very sense of identity thus acknowledges the fractured foundation in which colonialism is embedded – the annihilation of selves, juxtaposed with emancipatory visions. I couldn't help but land in the world trying to make sense of (and to redefine) how colonial structures shape our experience of the past, present, and future. Centuries later I find myself on a very different terrain from that of my ancestors (arts organizations, civic spaces, almost all levels of the educational framework – though predominantly colleges and universities) in which I find tools to map out my own journey of understanding.

Why is "EDI" in quotes?

Let me cut to the chase here. While I do a great deal of work in EDI spaces (trainings, conference sessions, movement building, my full time work outside of theater for that matter, etc.), I don't actually believe that EDI will save us from the violence of global white supremacy.

So to begin, I want to reflect on the trajectory of our field-wide vocabulary around the terms "equity, diversity, and inclusion" as they have been used within the context of movements toward justice in the United States before thinking about how a decolonizing framework might shift our collective thinking and practice.

"Diversity" has been thought of as a mixed composition (mostly) of bodies within an institutional space that creates opportunities for confrontation with difference. Briefly, after the Civil Rights Movement of the 1950s and 1960s, schools, colleges, and universities began creating institutional spaces for non-white students.[1] For the most part, ironically, due to the successes won by the Civil Rights Movement – which often perpetuate the false notion that racism has been conquered in the US – "diversity" in institutions is no longer sought after as a civil rights and justice issue. Instead, diversity is sought after for the purpose of increasing the economic value of institutions, which are still primarily owned and operated by white individuals. Leigh Patel, in her book *Decolonizing Educational Research*, puts it another way: "critiquing diversity as a concept too often desired to improve the institution through representation, through heuristics, not to fundamentally alter or dismantle the settler logics of white supremacy and heteropatriarchy."[2] The ideal of "diversity" has been divested of its radical power in the service of neoliberal goals.[3]

We see this pattern rehearsed in our field in a number of manifestations:

- The commodification of "equity, diversity, and inclusion" initiatives (think about the ways in which black and brown bodies are commodified in the name of "diversity"). As a personal example, a producer who was considering programming one of my plays once told me that my being both a woman and a person of color would "check more than one box" for the artistic director.
- Predominantly white institutions are receiving funding and prestige for "equity, diversity, and inclusion" work, while theaters of color continue to receive disproportionately low funding. This discrepancy is based largely on the capacity of the former to employ grant writers who can successfully complete the maddening application forms and insert the kind of measurable (colonizing) data that grantmakers are looking for.

For a broader discussion of the ways that colonial dynamics show up in the American theater, see "Decolonizing Theatre: An Introduction."[4]

Inclusion is an imperial project

The theorization and commodification of race in the US – making indigenous populations out to be just another one of several minority "races" within the broader US settler population – deliberately undermines the sovereignty of tribal nations for the purpose of the theft of tribal lands.[5] This has had a devastating effect, for which our field-wide effort at "equity, diversity, and inclusion" provides its own eerie rehearsal: a conceptual erasure of indigenous tribal and individual sovereignty for the purpose of an assumed collective mission (EDI). In other words, the concept and discourse around diversity actually serves to undermine contemporary indigenous peoples in the US and elsewhere.

The premise of any project of "inclusion" rests on the notion that there is a center that marginalized peoples should be drawn into. In this way, "inclusion" may be utilized as a less violent word for "assimilation." I've recently heard Keryl McCord[6] talk about the metaphor of the table. She reminds people that when practitioners talk about inclusion, they often ask *"whose voice is at the table?"* which isn't a bad question to ask. But "the table," according to Keryl, is white supremacy; it has an assumed authority all its own, an established system of discourse that qualifies those who are now allowed to speak and those who should be quiet. Its very imagined model does not depart from the white supremacist comfort zone.

I'd like to take a moment to build on the powerful work of Dr. Dafina-Lazarus Stewart,[7] who provided some framing questions for higher education workers to think about the difference between "diversity and inclusion" and "equity and justice" in an article in *Inside Higher Ed*. I'd like to push us into the language of decolonization. (Dr. Stewart's questions are in italics; my provocations follow.)

Colonial logics function on the premise that materials and knowledge should be drawn toward a stable center (empire), there to be transformed and then redistributed outward to the periphery (colony). The logics of colonialism are built on stratification and difference, but they always position the center as dominant.[8] Neoliberal research maintains the logics of stratification in order to frame its questions and then to hypothesize interventions. An intervention can "solve" a problem in the moment, but the system that creates the stratification in the first place is permitted to remain. How does this play out in theater institutions? For example, institution X identifies (or has been called out for) the fact that 90% of their resources (artistically or administratively) are only directed to straight white men. As an intervention to mitigate harm, they decide to initiate an "EDI Committee" with no institutional power, charging the committee with the task of creating an aspirational "EDI Statement." With no further work, the system that created the power differential to begin with is maintained. Even when EDI committees are given some power, they frequently have to struggle for institutional resources, legitimacy, and buy-in from colleagues. This maintains a colonial logics of stratification: EDI becomes a job with the same value as any other departmental role, rather than a liberatory guiding vision

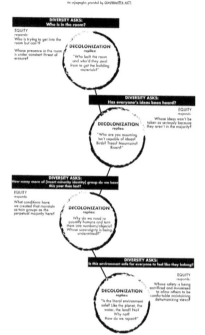

DIVERSITY vs EQUITY vs DECOLONIZATION

An infographic provided by GENAWAKEN ARTS

Diversity asks, "*Who's in the room?*" Equity responds: "Who is trying to get in the room but can't? Whose presence in the room is under constant threat of erasure?"

Decolonization responds, "Who built the room and who'd they steal from to get the building materials?"

Inclusion asks, "*Has everyone's ideas been heard?*" Justice responds, "Whose ideas won't be taken as seriously because they aren't in the majority?"

Decolonization responds, "Who are you assuming isn't capable of ideas? Birds? Trees? Mountains? Rivers?"

Diversity asks, "*How many more of [pick any minoritized identity] group do we have this year than last?*" Equity responds, "What conditions have we created that maintain certain groups as the perpetual majority here?"

Decolonization responds, "Why do we need to quantify humans and turn them into numbers/objects? Whose sovereignty is being undermined?"

Inclusion asks, "*Is this environment safe for everyone to feel like they belong?*" Justice challenges, "Whose safety is being sacrificed and minimized to allow others to be comfortable maintaining dehumanizing views?"

Decolonization responds, "Is the literal environment safe? Like the planet, the water, the land? No? Why not? How do we repair? And in claiming concern for others' safety, are we somehow assuming that we have the tools and the authority to fence off (and fence in) people, thus conceptually weaponizing some and victimizing others?"

for what kind of world we want to shape. It's also worth pointing out that, especially at predominantly white institutions, people of color, LGBTQIAs, and individuals with disabilities are often asked (and presumed to want) to serve on EDI committees without compensation for providing additional labor. This pattern also mimics the colonial dynamics of stratification by which individuals are first dehumanized and then implicitly or explicitly coerced into unpaid labor in service to the economic advancement of white supremacist institutions.

A decolonial alternative to research interventions is what Paulo Freire and Augusto Boal conceptualize as "praxis" or a continual and mutual process of action and critical reflection. I've heard my indigenous colleagues talk a great deal about reciprocity and relationality in art-making.[9] The ongoing and complementary cycle of reflexive action opens space for transformational process-based creative work. Performance pedagogies based on praxis are less concerned with inputs and outputs (that position artists and their work toward justice as objects of a capitalist system) and more concerned with process, dialogue, and encounter (that position artists as subjects and agents in their own art-making and liberation). A critical question for theater makers is how to manifest decolonial, praxis-based methodologies. What strategies are actually effective?

So what are the strategies?

In her work on decolonizing educational research, Patel calls on educational workers to pause, to halt the drive toward knowledge production, and to reflect on their relationship to the structures that perpetuate colonialist logics of ownership.[10] Similarly, as theater artists and dramaturgs we may pause in our work and reflect on our relationship to colonial systems, particularly in our work for "equity, diversity, and inclusion."

Systems instead of individualism

Many EDI initiatives begin from a point of interrogating individual identity. Training often begins with social location mapping exercises and developing vocabulary to identify (and possible responses for) individual instances of interpersonal oppression. Some programs and initiatives also help people understand the many ways we internalize oppressive practices and enact them ourselves. I've seen very few instances in the national theater landscape where EDI initiatives start from a systems-based approach to analyze and change the ways that institutions (both inside and outside the arts sector) interlock with one another to maintain colonial dynamics of oppression. I wonder what would happen if, as a field, we made a collective effort to understand the systems we've inherited. Start from systemic→ institutional→ interpersonal→ internalized, rather than from the opposite and more common trajectory.

Examine your relationship to the land

Here I want to rely on and amplify the work of my indigenous colleagues and collaborators who have been doing this work for many years, as really their voices should be centered in any discussion of how to acknowledge and get in right relationship to the lands on which we work and on which our institutions are built. The US Department of Arts and Culture, in consultation with and led by an extraordinary group of indigenous artists, has put together a fantastic resource on how to conduct land acknowledgments, called "Honor Native Land."[11] It's a wonderful starting place for people who are beginning to understand more about their relationship (you have one, whether you realize it or not) to indigenous lands and peoples.

A concrete strategy here would also obviously include hiring indigenous artists. I'd like to amplify the work that Spiderwoman Theatre, New Native Theatre, Native Voices at the Autry, Amerinda, Indigenous Direction, and Catalyst Dance, among many others, have been doing for decades. *American Theatre* magazine recently had an issue dedicated to native theater, including a list of over 100 artists currently working across the country.[12]

I'd also be curious to see what happens if we conceptualize the actual lands, waters, more-than-human beings, as part of our efforts toward collective liberation and justice. How do our art-making, our dramaturgy, and our institutions reflect the many interconnected relationships within which we exist and move?

Flatten hierarchies, dismantle borders, practice emergence

These three articulations are about looking for patterns in the structures of our relationships with one another and intentionally reshaping them toward collective liberation for all beings. Can we, as a field, begin to reshape the hierarchies we inhabit, moving them away from traditional top-down structures where power is disproportionately held by a very few individuals? Can we shape structures of decision-making that amplify everyone's individual agency in terms of the collective – in our organizations, our rehearsal rooms, our creative processes, our funding relationships, our relationships with audiences – in the way we think of the theatrical ecosystem altogether?

If you haven't read adrienne maree brown's important work, *Emergent Strategy*,[13] I'd highly encourage that as a starting place to gain more knowledge about principles of emergence.

Decolonization can often feel impossible because the very fabric of our society is embedded with colonial dynamics, but one aspect of emergence that I find particularly hopeful for this work is the fractal nature of the universe. A fractal pattern is one that repeats from very small scales to very large scales and occurs very commonly in nature, appearing in snowflake crystals, rivers, trees, the veins of leaves, seashells, hurricanes, and many other forms. For adrienne maree brown, the fractal pattern provides a template for how we might shift aspects of the world we shape and inhabit. Small changes in our day-to-day lives and relationships actually ripple outward in a fractal pattern and begin to shift the vast interconnected web of relations inside of which we exist. This has huge implications for all the ways our ideologies and philosophies around EDI are incongruous with our actions day-to-day. Emergence suggests that if we change small patterns (repairing harms in our individual relationships, building trust, accountability, and responsibility between ourselves and those around us, getting ourselves in right relationship with our local environments), these actions of repair have the capacity to ripple outward in a fractal pattern and begin to shape the world differently – toward justice and freedom. Emergence, I find, is fundamentally hopeful. It thinks both small and large at the same time, never losing focus of either.

I recently witnessed a beautiful example of emergence in action at the TCG Equity, Diversity, and Inclusion Institute Fall 2018 meeting in New York. During the meeting, Corinna Gus Schulenberg, TCG's director of communications and a core leader of the EDI Institute, introduced the cohort participants to Ravi Ragbir, an organizer with the New Sanctuary Coalition.[14] Ravi spoke powerfully to a room full of theater leaders about his experience as an undocumented immigrant and his encounters with ICE agents, and he provided concrete steps that institutional theaters can take to begin a sanctuary practice within their communities. Ravi's appearance at TCG's EDI Institute was made possible because Corinna and Ravi are personal friends whose lives touch one another in deep and meaningful ways.[15] I was inspired by the way Corinna followed emergent patterns in her own life and made the invitation for Ravi to speak with EDI Institute participants, rather than curating what could be considered a more traditional EDI training curriculum. I know the ripples of Ravi's session are still percolating in theaters across the country. Field-wide, we may ask ourselves: What are the ways that we draw borders around and within our institutions to separate ourselves from the communities and landscapes within which we are embedded? How might we begin to see (and expand) our artistic practice and our institutional buildings as existing not just in an artistic vacuum, but as deeply connected civic-cultural resources?

Value silence

A final strategy for decolonizing theater-making practice is developing a methodology that values silence. In a culture oversaturated with words, silence has become increasingly difficult not only to value but often even to find. And it is often devalued as a space of unsuccessful communication. In theater institutions, both artists and administrators are asked over and over to be productive (that is to say, literally to produce scripts, reports, sets, costumes, lines, blocking, and other proofs of productivity) in offices and rehearsal halls. I have found that practicing what I call "a pedagogy of silence" in institutional spaces can challenge the dominant discourse of production and open spaces for reflection. Importantly, silence allows time and space for observation of self and for encounter with others. A pedagogy of silence focuses attention not on the production and replication of artworks but on embodied encounters between beings in the process of creation.

Educators may consider creating spaces within their curricula for reflexive pauses (i.e. moments of silence) on a number of levels – pauses within the semester to personalize learning, pauses within a class session to elicit both reflection and analysis from students who might not otherwise speak up, and pauses within individual interactions with students for whole body listening and learning on the part of the educator. In Boal's games, particularly at the introductory level, participants do not use verbal language. Instead, participants are asked to pay attention to the information they give and receive with their bodies and to expand their physical choices beyond the learned rigidity of contemporary life – sitting at desks in the same posture all day long, typing on computers, or tapping screens. If participants can decrease their reliance on hyper-intellectualization, they may open the door to the profound wisdom of their own bodies. The often untapped knowledge stored in the bodies of people of color and people with other historically oppressed identities is especially deep. Therefore, as theater practitioners, perhaps we will want to re-think table-work in more interesting ways than simply interspersing it with "getting up on our feet"?

In any training session around EDI or decolonization that I have co-led, I try to make points of starting with silence, breath, and connection to the land. Often, my collaborators and I ask participants to begin by silently reflecting on their relationship to water, lands, or indigenous roots. I've found that this strategy helps to remove participants (and facilitators, for that matter) from the space of hyper-intellectual analysis that often accompanies EDI training, and instead silence sets a tone for connection to the deeply spiritual and personal work of decolonization.

I encourage anyone who might use the techniques I have discussed in this chapter to adapt them as needed to their own specific social and physical locations. Patel suggests, "Educational researchers who seek decolonial praxes would do well to remember, from their specific social locations and places, that knowledge is always place-specific."[16] I would love us to think about how the strategies suggested earlier might be situated within the coordinates of the epistemological and ontological lineages associated with our individual and institutional locations. These techniques can be used intentionally as a method of speaking back to and resisting the oppressive structures of neoliberalism as they manifest in theater institutions and elsewhere.

Finally, I leave off (because discussions of decolonization and EDI are never "done") with the hope that this chapter will open up new spaces that we all discover and create to contextualize our work in our own practice and in our own locations. On principle, in any workshop I give, I always end with a short game that signals not the end, but the new space that has been created for work to continue. In this game, with participants in a circle, I ask everyone to clap three times while counting out loud "one, two, three." However, on "three," the final clap never lands and we hold our hands apart. The silent clap and the space used to create it are reminiscent of the notion that, as Boal used to say, "the work never ends." We continue the work of moving toward a decolonized and more generative and just society. One, two . . .

Notes

1 In "How Desegregation Changed Us: The Effects of Racially Mixed Schools on Students and Society," a report published at Columbia University in the early 2000s, available online at www.tc.columbia.edu/faculty/asw86/faculty-profile/files/ASWells041504.pdf, Amy Stuart Wells et al. suggest that "school desegregation fundamentally changed the people who lived through it, yet had a more limited impact on the larger society. Public schools faced enormous challenges during the late 1970s as educators tried to facilitate racial integration amid a society that remained segregated in terms of housing, social institutions, and often employment. Nonetheless, desegregation made the vast majority of the students who attended these schools less racially prejudiced and more comfortable around people of different backgrounds. After high school, however, their lives have been far more segregated as they reentered a more racially divided society." The question of how universities were impacted through policies that sought to redress centuries of racial prejudice is a huge and many-faceted one, beyond the scope of this case study. But I want to acknowledge its importance to the wider issue of how diversity and inclusion began to have a voice in public discourse.

2 Patel, Leigh. *Decolonizing Educational Research: From Ownership to Answerability*. Routledge, New York (2016).

3 The work in this case study builds directly on a chapter called "Decolonizing 'diversity' on college campuses," which I contributed to *Applied Improvisation: Leading, Collaborating, & Creating Beyond the Theatre* (London: Bloomsbury, 2018).

4 Annalisa Dias and Madeline Sayet, "Decolonizing Theatre: An Introduction," *HowlRound*, May 27, 2018. Available online at https://howlround.com/decolonizing-theatrela-descolonizacion-del-teatro.

5 See Kim TallBear's extensive work on tribal belonging, DNA, and narratives of race. Available online at http://kimtallbear.com/pubs/.

6 Keryl McCord has more than thirty years of experience in the arts. She was formerly Operations Director at alternate ROOTS (https://alternateroots.org/) and is now the founder and CEO of Equity Quotient. Available online at https://artisticlogistics.org/consultants/.

7 Dafina-Lazarus Stewart, "Language of Appeasement," *Inside Higher Ed*, March 30, 2017. Available online at www.insidehighered.com/views/2017/03/30/colleges-need-language-shift-not-one-you-think-essay.

8 Linda Tuhiwai Smith, *Decolonizing Methodologies: Research and Indigenous Peoples* (New York: Zed Books; Dunedin: University of Otago Press, 1999).

9 See Paulo Freire, *Pedagogy of the Oppressed* (New York: Seabury Press, 1968). Additionally, see Augusto Boal's *Theatre of the Oppressed* (New York: Theatre Communications Group, 1985).

10 Patel, Leigh. *Decolonizing Educational Research: From Ownership to Answerability*. New York: Routledge (2016).

11 US Department of Arts and Culture, "Honor Native Land," 2018. Available online at https://usdac.us/nativeland/.

12 "A List of Native Theatres and Theatremakers," *American Theatre Editors*, March 20, 2018. Available online at www.americantheatre.org/2018/03/20/a-list-of-native-theatres-and-theatremakers/.

13 adrienne maree brown, *Emergent Strategy: Shaping Change, Changing Worlds* (Chico, CA: AK Press, 2017).

14 The New Sanctuary Coalition is an immigrants rights organization based in New York. See www.newsanctuarynyc.org/ for more information about sanctuary practice.

15 Corinna writes more about her friendship with Ravi in her blog. She speaks of how witnessing Ravi being forcefully arrested and detained by ICE agents in early 2018 directly influenced the process of her own coming-out as trans in this political moment: two lives deeply in relationship, yearning for justice and liberation, spinning fractal patterns outward into the universe. https://corinnaguschulenburg.com/2018/12/31/my-2018-in-review/.

16 Patel 2016: 94.

11 Dramaturging revolution

Diana Oh's *{my lingerie play} 2017: the concert and call to arms!!!!!!!!! the final installation*

Mei Ann Teo

Introduction

Columbus Circle in July 2017: where Diana and I meet for our first dramaturgy meeting. She looks at the script of the play I hold in my hand and asks, "What do I cut?" "I don't prescribe cuts," I say, "not at this point. Tell me first what you want this play to do – what action you want it to have in the world."[1] Diana then declares an ambitious vision, firmly rooted in understanding systemic oppression, one that demands accountability and longs for collective liberation. It's thrilling and exciting and just impossible enough for me to say YES! LET'S DO THIS! I also then realize: this is not a play. This is not an evening at the theater. This is a movement.

Diana Oh (she/they pronouns) is a queer Korean American performance artist/writer/actor/singer-songwriter/theatermaker/artist of color multi-hyphenate. Diana defies even those labels and descriptions, as they don't cover the activism, the leadership, the organizing, and the galvanizing force of her work. She strives to queer the world with her radical non-complacency. She's been performing/singing in her underwear as political action, manifesting as street installations with titles like "Installation 3/10: EVEN IF YOU FOUND ME LIKE THIS (you still can't rape me)," where she gathered a group of folks to lie down in their lingerie in the middle of Times Square with this sign framing them. Or "Installation 4/10: You were born from here," consisting of this text posted above a larger-than-scale clay sculpture of her vulva.

Diana's creations/installations began in 2014, performed in that year and created anew in 2017. The Ninth Installation of *The Concert and Call to Arms* in 2017 is the part that happens in the Rattlestick Theatre, which focuses the massive ambition of this work into the concision of a linear two-hour experience. The event also defies form, and, while it is just a slice in a lifetime of Diana's work, it holds the epic and intimate stories of how she has embraced being queered. It holds, in its multivalent forms, the celebrations and challenges and paradoxes of her experience: as Sara Holdren describes, it is "equal parts theater, punk rock concert, protest, confessional, and celebration."[2] It is a community space where dancing bursts forth, singing is accompanied by an entire audience blowing bubbles, and peeing when you need to is encouraged, despite the fact that one has to ascend the stage to get to the bathroom. It is a space where folks respect gender pronouns, where caring is cool, and where agency and do-no-harm exist in sweet balance. It also holds furious anger. The space turns, quite literally, into a barber shop where a volunteer might get their head shaved. And how it feels? It feels like a wide-open field of poppies for frolicking while unabashedly fighting our innermost shame demons. It also feels like a celebratory, debaucherous church.

This case study will cover the process and issues arising in the dramaturgy of *The Concert and Call to Arms* – this 2017 iteration being my lingerie play – to be referred to as {mlp}. It opened at the Rattlestick Theatre in New York City's West Village in September 2017.

Figure 11.1 Diana Oh at Rattlestick Theatre, 2018

Source: Photography credit Carla Vega

Dramaturgy

First, it is of utmost importance to acknowledge that everyone who worked on the piece, as well as the audience, participated in the dramaturgy of this production. It was not a role solely held by the dramaturg, nor was it a finite process. We were a living, breathing web of interstitial experiences and bodies that, together, held the work to the light. The co-director Orion Johnstone, the entire creative design team, the musicians, the producers, the crew, the artistic director Daniella Topol, and also the audience: all of us were involved in how this was built, to a much greater extent than I'd previously experienced in theater-making. This is central to the dramaturgy of revolution – the understanding and value of the interconnectedness of everyone. Dramaturgical process is understood as "how one thing leads to another." Dramaturgy toward revolution recognizes that it takes collective actions, how we build upon each other and segue from each other: and how this extent of fluidity requires communal knowledge and support.

In *Emergent Strategy*, adrienne maree brown writes about how we shape change and move toward collective liberation through studying nature's patterns and resilience strategies. She uses Nick Obolenksy's definition of emergence: "Emergence is the way complex systems and patterns arise out of a multiplicity of relatively simple interactions." She then offers, "Emergence is beyond what the sum of its parts could even imagine."[3] In these concepts I find the way that theater, as a series of interactions and choices, then offers up an alternative system and pattern that subverts our inherited reality of systemic violence. In {mlp}, we can see these relatively simple actions and choices construct resistance to accepted and often complacent norms.

For instance, let's look at the dramaturgy behind the title of our piece. In Zhailon Levingston's interview with Diana published in *The Brooklyn Rail*, he asks, "Can you explain the significance of the number nine for you as it relates to your show?" Diana replies: "There are nine exclamation points in the title because it's the ninth installation. Nine exclamation points because we are taking up as much space as we want."[4]

This explanation reveals the dramaturgy of agency that Diana is calling forth as a tool for change. Not only are the exclamation points expressive of the title and the explosiveness of the event, they also physically and visually challenge the notion of "title" itself as definitive and integrative signifier. It's also proof that the title did its job, as it was called "too much" in a *New York Times* article "So, You're Going to Call Your Play _____?," whose entire purpose was to shame titles that weren't "efficient."[5] Indeed, I'd add to this: nine is a number that has powerful connotations across cultures and religions. Nine, as the highest single-digit number (in base ten), symbolizes completeness in the Bahá'í faith. In Christianity, Christ died at the ninth hour of the day to make the way of salvation open to everyone. The Jewish Day of Atonement, Yom Kippur, considered by many to be the holiest day of the year, begins at sunset on day nine of the seventh Hebrew month. In the space of those nine exclamation points we invited our audiences to replenish themselves with all of the associations they accorded to that number.

Diana's practice of resilience and revolution is to claim the agency of her body/mind/spirit/heart, while honoring her guts and instincts, as they are connected to a deeper truth than our over-stimulated brains are aware of. "I do what I want on that stage." And that is a revolutionary act, to see a queer woman of color – who is Korean American – get to be "doing what I want on that stage."[6] By allowing for no separation between herself and her art, she practiced being fully honest and present in all interactions. It encouraged genuine inclusivity amongst the collaborators and the audience as well. We were invited into a space, set up intentionally with co-director Orion Johnstone, in which our bodies and how they felt were honored as vital to decision-making, vital to the dramaturgy of the work. In describing the set – "everything was ripped from my journal" – Diana declares her hope that

> people walk away feeling like they have complete and total agency to act and speak out and honor themselves and honor their truth and honor their power. That any time they feel that urge to [say], "I feel like I can do something but I don't know if it's like this, and I don't know . . ." they [respond to themselves], "You can. . . . And you must. You just have to put one foot in front of the other to do it."[7]

Process

As Grace Lee Boggs has suggested, we must transform ourselves to transform the world.[8] For {mlp} the choosing of decision-makers – and how the work of their life was part and parcel of the journey – had utmost importance. Diana says this about Orion Johnstone, co-director:

> Everyone should work with a sex coach on an art piece at least once in their lives. Orion is a sex and relationship life coach, liberator, co-conspirator, activist, highly collaborative, superqueero. They [Orion] hold us accountable. I trust them with all the sides of me that certain rooms have made me feel ashamed of.[9]

In *Stage and Candor*, Orion says:

> As a sexuality educator, I am passionate about not just inviting indi-
> viduals to transcend shame, but deepening all of our understandings
> of how our personal shame is connected to intersecting and overlap-
> ping systems of oppression. . . . The invitation that Diana posed to me,
> essentially, is how do we live by those central questions, to embody
> our commitment to the idea that *how* we make is as important as *what*
> we make?[10]

Each member of the team was invited to bring their whole selves to
the process. Our stage manager, Jhanaë Bonnick, participating in rehearsal
room "sermons" where she told us about her storytelling roots, also ended
up speaking in the show. Because Diana didn't want to be the only non-
binary or queer person in the band, Rocky Vega learned the bass for the
show. Victor Cervantes, as the associate producer at Rattlestick, brought an
incredible wealth of knowledge and connection to the queer community.

The growth of {mlp} involved listening to each other with intention. For
instance, in one of my first sessions with Diana, we spoke about a section in
the play where she talked about how we are affected by the language of our
leaders. I related this to the analogy of spellcasting, which was a metaphor and
reality with which Diana and Orion resonated in relationship to queer magic.
Orion then asked Diana to find the structure of the work in terms of spells that
she's casting, providing a platform for the magic that happened in the show.

Dramatic structure toward revolution

In {mlp}, Diana says: "What 'Queer the World' means to me is *not* that
everyone should be gay. 'Queer the World' is direct confrontation, an
unapologetic disruption of the lies that capitalist patriarchal cis heteronor-
mative society would tell us." There were two particular learning moments
that I'd like to share, relating to decentering whiteness and lifting up anti-
rape culture. I love the tenets set out by the Vedic Sutras about good theater:
entertain the drunk – which I think of as engaging those who go to theater
not to learn but be entertained, revealing the way the world works and
showing us how to live. In its pure celebration and joyful disruption, its
music, dance, and freedom of aesthetics, Diana Oh's piece gloriously enter-
tains the drunk. In most theater, revealing the way the world works is often
at the center – via drama and conflict. Showing us how to live is done less
frequently, and I'd like to put forward that it is most important when we are
crafting dramatic structure toward revolution.

Decentering whiteness

In the context of American theater, which is predominantly white, Diana says that her work as a Korean American performance artist is made specifically to resist, to retaliate, and to make space for more bodies of color. And yet, at a point in the rehearsal process, we as a team had to grapple with a moment in the play in which she wanted to have a song performed with all people of color on the stage. Ryan McCurdy, a close collaborator of Diana's and the actor/drummer in the show, is also a white cis man. Diana suggested a moment where Ryan would apologize on behalf of white men: a form of ritual cleansing. But we started to question what it would mean for Ryan to take this on, given the shift it would mean for him from ally to apologist. Moreover, Diana's asking him to apologize might take away the authenticity of an apology, and the apology itself would pull focus from the central event of all POC's rocking-out on stage.

This opened up a larger discourse of how we navigate white accountability, agreeing that it is important but then also asking what amount of space such grappling with whiteness should take up in {mlp}; after all, this is a play about Diana's queering, not about white men inviting us to join them in checking in with themselves. We cut the apology, having Ryan simply hand over the drumsticks to Diana. Through this evocative action we chose to model the way white co-conspirators can step aside to allow for the necessary event of uplifting people of color to take what they (white people) had formerly seen as "their" place.

Anti-rape culture

In {mlp}, Diana shares an experience about being cat-called by a carload of men late at night. In the rehearsal process, she then invited a moment of audience participation, asking the audience to speak out about what they themselves had experienced on the street. The idea was to hear and collectively hold this pain so that we could acknowledge the state of daily violence and harassment that occurs and is so often dismissed as not "qualifying" for "trauma" status. Diana would then sing an incredibly tender ballad, a balm, a way in which we might heal together. That was the hope, at least. After one of our full runs, Kate McGee, our lighting designer (who is transfeminine), said, "Not a week goes by when my life is not threatened in the street. Can this play hold that?"

Kate's question opened up a powerful discussion of what a play can hold – what is our duty to our audience in asking them to relive trauma, and what is the cost of that to them? And for what purpose? What is exploitative? How do we make work that represents anti-rape culture and yet also be sensitive to survivors, holding all the rest of us accountable?

On a parallel track, Orion had asked Diana to do some writing on what she was experiencing in the making of the 2017 iteration and what was new to her this time around. She wrote that this was the first time that she was doing the show while single. I immediately thought about her unabashed sex-positivity, and how fun it would be if she invited an audience member to make out with her every night. Orion then framed this as an enthusiastic consent workshop: Diana would ask for a volunteer who would like to make out with her, being prepared to step through the process of checking in with their two bodies. Throughout the process, Diana and the audience member would feel able and encouraged to say "no" and "yes" in any moment. Here again, we found a model of how we might wish the world to be, opening up ways to show how we can be transparent, thoughtful, and brave in our vulnerable, sexy, and intimate relationships, letting go of the need for conquest or submission that is so profoundly linked to shame.

Conclusion

The humble act of dramaturgy, in the service of revolution, is the revolution itself. It is in these choices, seemingly small and insignificant, that we are able to reflect deeply upon assumptions and paradigms. In order to dismantle shame culture, we commit first to wrestle with shame within ourselves. We disrupt oppressive ideologies first through decolonizing our own imaginations. We gather a community to listen to, to be trauma-informed and healing-centered. These personal and private practices are the root of change and transformation for the communal space of the theater.

Acknowledgments

The installations would not have been possible without the help and support of producer Michelle Stern, videographer Jon Burklund, community engagement with Nathaniel Claridad and Anthony Ritosa, and social media with Corey Ruzicano, Rattlestick, Venturous Capital Grant, and the TOW Foundation.

Notes

1 Conversation, July 2017.

2 "Diana Oh Is a Fierce Feminist Who Rocks Out in Her Underwear," available online at www.vulture.com/2017/10/diana-oh-is-a-fierce-feminist-who-rocks-out-in-her-underwear.html.
3 adrienne maree brown, *Emergent Strategy* (Chico, CA: AK Press, 2017), 13.
4 "Nine Questions for Diana Oh," available online at https://brooklynrail.org/2017/10/theater/Nine-Questions-for-Diana-Oh.
5 "So, You're Going to Call Your Play _____?," available online at www.nytimes.com/2018/08/10/theater/plays-titles-the-new-one.html.
6 "How One Actor Turned her Brush With Street Harassment into a Raucous Emotional Concert," available online at www.upworthy.com/how-one-actor-turned-her-brush-with-street-harassment-into-a-raucous-emotional-concert?
7 Ibid.
8 See interview with Jenny Hollander, "To Make a Revolution, People Must Not Only Struggle Against Existing Institutions. They Must Make a Philosophical/Spiritual Leap and Become More 'Human' Human Beings. In Order to Change/Transform the World, They Must Change/Transform Themselves," – *Living for Change*. Available online at www.bustle.com/articles/115047-9-grace-lee-boggs-feminist-quotes-that-will-inspire-you-to-smash-through-the-glass-ceiling.
9 Ibid.
10 "A Conversation with Orion Stephanie Johnstone," available online at https://stageandcandor.com/conversations/orion-johnstone/-.W-78MpNKiRs.

Cultural landscapes, past, present, and future

12 The stakes of expanding a cultural landscape

Dramaturging, adapting, and performing Gao Xinjian's *The Other Shore*

Walter Byongsok Chon

The Other Shore is different from conventional drama. One of the differences is that the play does not attempt to put together a coherent plot. I only intend it to be a revelation, to portray some of life's experiences and feelings in a pure dramatic form, i.e., in the same way that music is pure.

– Gao Xingjian

Gao Xingjian's play *The Other Shore* presents an allegorical and abstract journey, from the materialized world to the nonexistent place, from fullness to emptiness, from everything to nothing, and from here to the other shore.[1] The play was originally scheduled to premiere at the Beijing People's Art Theatre in 1986. However, one month into rehearsal they suspended the play, fearing that the theme of the individual versus the collective might upset the Communist government and invite official sanctions. Xingjian had served as resident playwright there since the Chinese government assigned him that position in 1981. Yet his non-realistic form and metaphysical themes did not adhere to the "acceptable" Stanislavkian realism and socialist doctrines advocated by the company and immediately aroused the authorities' suspicions. The consequences of a government sanction were severe. When Xingjian, along with the director Lin Zhaohua, revived his first play, *Bus Stop*, as a "rehearsal" in 1983 (the company originally declined the play in 1981) – he was barred from publication for one year and was almost sent to a labor camp to "receive training."

Xingjian left the Beijing People's Art Theatre in 1987. In the Communist regime of China, where it was customary for the Communist party to assign artists to institutions, his departure meant a permanent break from his homeland. Yet he found a second home in France. He directed *The Other Shore* in Taiwan in 1990 and in Hong Kong in 1995 and was awarded the Nobel

Prize in Literature for his entire body of work in 2000. In his Nobel lecture, "The Case for Literature": "Literature transcends ideologies, national boundaries and racial consciousness in the same way that the individual's existence basically transcends this or that ism. This is because man's existential condition is superior to any theories or speculations about life." Despite his international accolades, he is still not widely known in his home country of China.

I came across Xingjian's work in 2009 as an MFA student at Yale School of Drama's Dramaturgy and Dramatic Criticism program, while preparing for my qualifying exam on the topic of Theater of the Absurd. I was surprised when I learned that Xingjian's play *Bus Stop* (1981), which I read as an international example of Theater of the Absurd in the manner of Beckett and Ionesco, was accused of being anti-socialist and was forced to close at the Beijing People's Art Theatre in 1983, preluding the fate of *The Other Shore* a few years later. *Bus Stop*, to put it succinctly, depicts a group of people waiting for a bus, which will probably not come. Yet they wait, talk about their lives with each other, and talk about waiting. There was something particularly haunting about the portrayed situation, which could happen anywhere yet would acquire different significance and interpretation depending on the time, the location, and the identity and status of the people waiting, none of which is specified in the play. The characters are simply introduced as "Old Man," "Girl," "Silent Man," and "Mother," to list a few, with only their ages specified. The apparent similarity to *Waiting for Godot* established Xingjian's connection with Theater of the Absurd.

Martin Esslin, in the first publication of *The Theatre of the Absurd* (1961), grouped several European playwrights who had emerged after World War II under this title, attributing their similarities in theme and form to their disillusionment with rationality and common sense after the devastation of two world wars. These writers, including Beckett, Adamov, Ionesco, and Genet, share the theme of a "sense of metaphysical anguish at the absurdity of the human condition" and express it formally through "the open abandonment of rational devices and discursive thought."[2] On the one hand, the term "Theater of the Absurd" became widely accepted to designate the works of these playwrights. On the other hand, Esslin's reading of the shared tendencies in these plays as reflecting the writers' common response to the political situation also became highly debated and even dismissed by playwrights he had grouped in this category. At issue was the discrepancy between intention and reading/reception; while the aftermath of the war was the historical context in which these plays were written, it is open to question as to whether or to which degree the plays' form and subject matter directly reflected or responded to this context. Xingjian's *Bus Stop* suffered from a similar discrepancy between intention and reception. Xingjian, a student of Meyerhold, Mayakovsky, Brecht, Beckett, and Ionesco, intended to write apolitical "cold literature" with *Bus Stop*. Yet for Xingjian, writing in Communist China, the play was not received that way. Its portrayal of a state of doubt made it, in the eyes of the government, anti-socialist; hence the enforced closure. Its non-realistic form also went against the aesthetic of the Beijing People's Art Theatre, which was deeply committed to realism and the Stanislavskian method of acting.

The question of how a play's reception and interpretation change in view of historical context was particularly intriguing to me as an international dramaturg now working in the US When fellow Yale dramaturg Cheng-Han Wu approached me in 2010 and asked me to be the dramaturg for *The Other Shore* for a Yale Cabaret production under his direction, I was immediately drawn to the question: How would this play, which was more disjointed than *Bus Stop* and barely known in the US, be received in the context of Yale, New Haven, the East Coast, and the US? The particular history of the play and the playwright brought up more questions about the prospect of our production: How would the historical background be most usefully framed within the dramaturgical material I intended to provide for the audience? How would the playwright's Nobel Prize impact the reception of the play? How would this play, written by a Chinese playwright, appeal to different identities and ethnicities? And how might our production, together with my dramaturgical material, enrich the theatrical and cultural experience of the audience?

As a dramaturg from South Korea, I was, first of all, thrilled at the opportunity to introduce a play from a neighboring Asian country to mostly western students and patrons. I understood that even for the Yale Cabaret, which was run by Drama School students and was a site for student-driven and experimental work, Xingjian's play was going to be a unique offering. I immediately started my work as production dramaturg with comprehensive research so that the creative team, which had yet to be assembled, would understand not only the historical and cultural context but also the particular form and the Buddhist philosophy embedded in the play.[3] To familiarize the audience with the history and the context of the play, I wrote a thorough spread of dramaturgy notes in the program, which included information about the author's life, the play's premiere and its subsequent production history, and excerpts from Xingjian's Nobel Prize lecture. Yet the ensemble-based form of the play and our particular rehearsal circumstances demanded that my dramaturgical role go beyond the research and the writing and expand to adapting the piece and, to my surprise, acting in it.

In the Yale Cabaret calendar, which offers a new production every weekend, our performance was scheduled from November 11 to 13, 2010, with

Figure 12.1 Marcus Henderson, Babak Gharaei-Tafti, Walter Byongsok Chon, Baibing
       Chen, and Jillian Taylor, from left to right, in *The Other Shore*, directed by
       Cheng-Han Wu, Yale Cabaret

Source: Photography credit Nick Thigpen

two performances each day at 8pm and 11pm. *The Other Shore* was slated
to broaden the cultural and theatrical landscape as a play from an underrep-
resented culture with a distinctive voice and form. Huei Li Leow, the stage
manager who eventually also served as choreographer for this piece, recollects her pride in the unique contribution this play made: "Bringing an Eastern play that had been banned in China to the Yale Cabaret stage was in and of
itself a statement of diversity."[4] Diversity was also reflected in the makeup of
the cast and creative team. Director Wu recollects: "Most of the collaborators
were from different countries, including the US, Taiwan, Hong Kong, South
Korea, and Singapore. Culturally and ethnically diverse, the creative team
mirrored the small society formed by multiple interpersonal relationships
appearing in Xingjian's play (see Figure 12.1)."[5] Wu deliberately gathered
designers from Asian countries to express the expanse of Xingjian's visual
and aural world, which could form a dialogue with the mixed ethnicities

in the cast that had been assembled by accident and availability. The set designer Wiki Lo, from China, attributes her inspiration for the almost-bare stage with minimum props to the philosophy embedded in the play: "The text reflects the primacy of emptiness prevalent in Eastern aesthetics. The stage picture evokes a blank canvas, where words are a presence in an abstract painting rather than a functional narrative device."[6]

The original text requires at least sixteen characters, an impossible number to recruit in the middle of a hectic semester at Yale School of Drama. Wu and I cut and adapted the text for five performers, and our assembled cast consisted of a Caucasian woman (Jillian Taylor), an Iranian American man (Babak Gharaei-Tafti), an African American man (Marcus Henderson), a Chinese man (Baibing Chen), and, because we could not find the fifth performer, myself as a South Korean man.

As written, the play does not have any scene breaks but moves seamlessly from situation to situation, from a playful game to scenes of tense conflict to profound self-exploration. In our adaptation, we focused on clarifying the stages of this journey by creating twelve scenes that staged an allegorical journey from the birth of consciousness to the confrontation of mortality. We also needed to be conscious of the length of our adaptation so as to keep the performance under sixty minutes, the maximum length of a performance at the Yale Cabaret. The original thirty-eight pages in our edition were cut to twenty-eight pages. A few scenes were staged solely with movement, choreography, and music. Eventually our production came to be about fifty minutes long.

The play starts with a Prologue, where all five performers are anxiously engaged in their daily lives, such as having a fight with a partner or looking for a missing dog. The Prologue shifts into a slow movement, which comes to a stop as two "Rope Players" appear with a rope: "Here's a rope. Let's play a game, but we've got to be serious, as if we're children playing their game."[7] The rope play establishes the many kinds of relationships that can exist among people, depending on how they are linked and where power lies; in so doing, it challenges the boundaries between "mature" concerns and those retrospectively patronized as "child's play," reminding audiences that all power relationships can be experienced with utter seriousness no matter what the context. The rope transforms into a river, which everyone tries to cross to get to the other shore. After a struggle on the river, they all faint. Whether they have reached the other shore is open to question. A Woman wakes them up, but they have lost not only their memories but also their language. The Woman teaches the Crowd, using gestures: "This is a hand." The more language the Crowd picks up, the more violent they get, leading to one member saying, "I'll kill you."

At this point, the Young Man emerges as the protagonist. After confrontations with his father who demands obedience and with his mother who urges him to start a family, he goes to a party. A woman is killed there, and he is framed for the murder, which leads him to embark on a journey on his own. He encounters the Crowd in different situations, where he experiences and observes the injustices done to the individual who stands up to the Crowd. He runs away defeated, until he is left alone to face his shadow:

MAN: Who are you?
SHADOW: Your heart.

The original text ends with the performers gradually breaking out of their roles, from being in a dreamlike state – "I dreamed that there's a place of ivory in my stomach, it scared me to death!" – to dismissing the performance as illusion and returning to a meta-reality: "What kind of stupid play is this anyway? Are you doing anything tomorrow?"[8] However, rather than ending the Man's journey either in defeat or as a dream, we decided to extend the journey into infinity, allowing the play to end with the journey as a continuous process. At the close, the Man hears his Mother's voice again: "Do you still remember me? You've almost forgotten me, haven't you? I only know we should go forward, is that right? Is that right? Is that right?" In the original text, the Mother's words appear in an earlier scene, but we moved it to the end to show that the Man was driven, whether he knows it or not, by his own history. In the last image in our production, the Man is left between two interfacing mirrors at each end of the stage, creating infinite reflections. Left naked, he runs away toward one set of mirrors, which open up a path for him. As he disappears, simultaneously his Shadow runs in from the other set of mirrors. Then there is darkness.

Several questions remain in the end. Is the Man still searching for enlightenment (the other shore)? Is he running away? Or is he caught in an endless loop? Wu traces the inspiration for the last image to a discussion with me: "When I was frustrated about the direction of the play, Chon mentioned 'Maybe the other shore is this shore, and this shore is the other shore,' a cyclical perspective that matches my research interest, my worldview, and my philosophy of life."[9] In this respect, the Man's journey was far from over.

By the time Wu and I finished the adaptation and assembled four performers, the opening was less than two weeks away. Our short rehearsal period forced us to focus on completing the staging of the various kinds of scenes and did not leave us much time to contemplate how the piece would be received and interpreted. For his swift and straightforward way of prescribing the blocking, the performers jokingly called Wu "dictator-director," ironically indicating the very political circumstance Xingjian had originally been accused of criticizing at the play's Chinese premiere. Yet most scenes with the Crowd still required a devised and democratic approach because the lines were not attached to specific characters. We also needed to establish the relationships among the members of the Crowd as well as the particular group dynamics of the Crowd. As dramaturg/performer, I designed an exercise that would help us build a foundation for each character as crowd members in various situations. I made small pieces of paper with one or two crowd lines for each scene and put them in a bag. The performers, including myself, walked around the room. Any one of us would reach into the bag and pick a random piece of paper. The task for that performer was to immediately say the line to each of us with the objective of convincing us to listen to him/her. This exercise helped us to establish our particular group dynamic as well as our individual impacts on one another. I assigned the Crowd's lines based on our discovery from this exercise: Babak Gharaei-Tafti became the Man, and the rest of us shared many roles, including Woman, Father, Mother, Shadow, and Stable Keeper.

The production expressed the world as one that could both reflect specific Chinese culture and could be widely valid for many cultures. Instead of offering the audience our interpretation, we deliberately created a fragmented and evocative world, not only within the text but also in the production elements. The five performers were clad all in white to suggest our common nature as humans while also intimating our individuality underneath. The stage was bare and long, with the audience seats and dinner tables on each long side. This intimate arrangement enabled a direct interaction between stage and stalls, and, in a few Crowd scenes, members of the audience were called upon to fill the stage as Crowd members. We moved around white wooden boxes to indicate different locations. The soundscape was part of the immersive atmosphere we were aiming for. The sound designer and composer Junghoon Pi was on stage the whole time, playing live instruments while operating the sound system. Pi, who is from South Korea, recalls:

> I played just a few musical instruments, mainly percussion, to keep [the music and the sound] as minimal as possible, because creating the sense of 'void' was more important in this piece than filling the space with something. This is a common philosophy in East Asia.[10]

In the mirror dance right before the Man faces his Shadow, each of the performers held the mirrors up to the audience members so that they could see a reflection of themselves. Our intention was that they would not only see the journey of the Man but also have the same opportunity for self-reflection as does the Man at the end of his journey.

The audience received our production with great enthusiasm but with many different responses. Thanks to our marketing team's efforts there were more Asian patrons than usual, who expressed how glad they were to see a play that had emerged from their own culture. Huei Li remembers one Caucasian patron calling the performance "dissonant" and "trippy" because it offered her something unexpected and unfamiliar.[11] A couple of high school teachers approached Wu and me and asked about our process and artistic choices. They were going to teach this play in their school soon afterwards. Upon digesting the various responses, I was reminded of my own initial curiosity of how this play would be received in a different historical context. The stark contrast between the suppression of the play by the Beijing People's Art Theatre on account of the "politically sensitive" theme in 1986 and the open embrace of our production by the Yale and New Haven community in 2010 demonstrated not only how a play's reading could drastically shift under different historical and political circumstances but also how thoughtful and daring artistic choices could open up the production's interpretive possibilities. I also wondered (and this question inevitably remains unanswered) how *The Other Shore* would have played to the Yale audience in its original form with all fifteen characters.

When Wu and I embarked on this project, we neither intended to make a statement on diversity nor were we concerned about how different or unfamiliar our production would be for the community in which we staged it. We believed in the artistic value of the play and were confident that our production would offer a rich theatrical experience. The diverse identities of the creative team and the cast brought in many different perspectives. It was intriguing to see that our experiences with this piece were widely different. To Wu and me, this kind of storytelling was nothing out of the ordinary: the fragmentary narrative correlates with the complementary coexistence of presence and void, dark and light, and the yin and yang in Eastern philosophy. Our production theatricalized this philosophy, using the bodies of the performers and the design elements. A focus on process rather than destination, a constant search for the incomprehensible, and the eventual uncertainty and metaphysical anguish, are embedded in the dramaturgy of the piece. A couple of American cast members who were acting in a play from Asia for the first time admitted at the talkback that they were still trying to figure out what this play was about. Their response was oddly satisfying to me because it meant that we had succeeded in maintaining the philosophical core of the piece. Performing the triple duties of dramaturg, adapter, and actor, I realized how my training, cultural background, and identity could be optimized in a piece close to my own culture. My identity as a South Korean obtained more significance in this production, which required a profound reach to understand the specific philosophy and the cultural sentiment of my own roots.

Critically recollecting the Yale Cabaret production of *The Other Shore* affirmed for me that our effort contributed to a more diverse and inclusive theatrical and cultural landscape at the Yale School of Drama and the city of New Haven, Connecticut. The eager responses from Cheng-Han Wu, now in Taiwan; Wiki Lo, now in China; Huei Li Leow, now in New Orleans; and Junghoon Pi, now in South Korea, to my request for their reflection on their experiences with *The Other Shore*, affirm that they continue to share my belief as well. If we could remount this production I would consider further exploring the fragmentary nature of self and identity embedded in Buddhist philosophy by rotational or even random casting of the major roles. In our production, the Man was played by Babak Gharaei-Tafti, an Iranian American performer. But what if, with more rehearsal time and resources, we rotated the performers so that the Man was played by an African American,

Figure 12.2 Walter Byongsok Chon, Dramaturging the new play Three Views of the Same Object by the late Henry Murray at the Great Plains Theatre Conference, 2012

Source: Photography credit Thomas Grady

a Chinese, a Korean, a Caucasian, or a performer of any other identity? The fluid casting across gender and ethnicity would challenge the western notion of self as an intact entity and would invoke the Buddhist philosophy of reincarnation. The audience would experience even further complication if one could watch two performances in a row (which would be possible given the short running time), with the cast playing different characters the second time around. The implication for cultural representation as well as the scope of the audience experience would expand immensely, like two mirrors facing each other.

Notes

1 The original title *Bi'an* literally translates to "the other shore" or "the shore on the other side" and refers to *paramita*, the land of enlightenment in Buddhism.
2 Martin Esslin, *The Theatre of the Absurd*, 3rd ed. (New York: Vintage Books, 2004), 23–24.
3 The dramaturgy packet included essays from *The Other Shore: Plays by Gao Xingjian* (Hong Kong: The Chinese University Press, 1999), Sy Ren Quah's *Gao Xingjian and Transcultural Chinese Theater* (Honolulu, HI: University of Hawaii Press, 2004), Jessica Yeung's *Ink Dances in Limbo: Gao Xingjian's Writing as Cultural Translation* (Hong Kong: Hong Kong University Press, 2008), and Xingjian's Nobel Prize lecture "The Case for Literature."
4 Conversation by email, February 26, 2018.
5 Conversation by email, February 28, 2018.
6 Conversation by email, April 28, 2018.
7 The text is from our adaptation. The original source material is Gao Xingjian, *The Other Shore: Plays by Gao Xingjian*, trans. Gilbert C. F. Fong (Hong Kong: The Chinese University Press, 1999), 1–44.
8 Xingjian, *The Other Shore*, 40–41.
9 Conversation by email, February 28, 2018.
10 Conversation by email, March 4, 2018.
11 Conversation by email, February 26, 2018.

13 Visit to a zoot planet
UCSC suits up in 2017

Michael M. Chemers

What makes *Zoot Suit* more than a museum piece, especially a production done at a university theater? The play's 1978 premiere by the Center Theatre Group at the Mark Taper Forum in Los Angeles was wildly popular. At that time, the play was not only a stern rebuke to mainstream US society for its lingering refusal to allow Mexican Americans full participation in the so-called American Dream but also a vibrant celebration of an Other-Than-Anglo vision of what it meant to be an American. Luis Valdez's vision was as uniquely and authentically "about" Americans as the visions represented in the plays of Eugene O'Neill, Tennessee Williams, Arthur Miller, and Lilian Hellman but (thanks to differences in language, style, and experiences) remained barely recognizable *as* American at all to mainstream audiences. As a result, the play became engaged in some powerful political commentary, most notably through the character of "El Pachuco." ("Forget the war overseas, carnal. Your war is on the home front," El Pachuco remarks wryly of his struggle to be seen, acknowledged, and accepted by his doubtful countrymen and women.)

Pachuchismo refers to a particular subset of Chicanx culture present in Los Angeles, particularly prominent in the 1930s and 40s. Pachuco culture originates among Mexican descendants living in El Paso, Texas (also known as Chuco, or "filthy," Town, hence *para El Chuco*) and Ciudad Juaréz, Mexico. In his 1967 *Labyrinth of Solitude*, Octavio Paz writes of pachucos that:

> What distinguishes them, I think, is their furtive, restless air: they act like persons who are wearing disguises, who are afraid of a stranger's look because it could strip them and leave them stark naked. . . . This spiritual condition, or lack of a spirit, has given birth to a type known as the pachuco. The pachucos are youths, for the most part of Mexican origin, who form gangs in southern cities; they can be identified by

their language and behaviour as well as by the clothing they affect. They are instinctive rebels, and North American racism has vented its wrath on them more than once. But the pachucos do not attempt to vindicate their race or the nationality of their forebears. Their attitude reveals an obstinate, almost fanatical will-to-be, but this will affirms nothing specific except their determination . . . not to be like those around them.[1]

One marker of pachuco culture, adopted by both men and women of the era, was the zoot suit. "Zoot" is jazz slang meaning "worn or performed in an exaggerated style," and the suit (with its long finger-tip jacket, wide lapels, high-waisted, full-cut trousers, elaborate vests, wide-collared shirt, and wide-brimmed hat) was popularized by jazz-age Harlem fashionistas and was quickly picked up as a status symbol by young men and women of many ethnic minorities, including Jews, Latinos, and Filipinos. To a 21st-century eye, the zoot suit seems stylish but quaint: lost to us is the powerful and dangerous political statement the suit made. After the bombing of Pearl Harbor in 1941, the US Office of Price Administration began to ration commodities they deemed necessary to the war effort, including fabric. Zoot suits were expensive and illegal to sell – they could be acquired as alterations only from bootleg tailors – and in the popular media the zoot suit became associated with enemies of the state. The zoot suit became a target for a rising xenophobic belief that minorities, perhaps all minorities, were secret agents of the Axis working to destroy America from within.

This xenophobia peaked with the Zoot Suit Riots – a week-long series of events beginning May 30, 1943, in which large cohorts of white servicemen left their stations in Los Angeles, armed with clubs, to brutally assault zoot suiters and strip them of their regalia. Police refused to interfere, and after the violence they arrested the zoot suiters, praising the servicemen as "vigilantes." Eventually, the servicemen began assaulting minorities whether they were wearing zoot suits or not. On June 8, the Los Angeles City Council attempted to address the problem by banning zoot suits, but copycat riots occurred in Chicago, San Diego, Detroit, Philadelphia, and New York. These riots and the utter failure of the US Justice System to provide sufficient redress for their victims inspired a generation of civil rights leaders, including a young zooter pimp called Detroit Red (later known as Malcolm X).

This was the politically-charged environment in which the Sleepy Lagoon murder trials occurred. Enrique Reyes Leyvas, known to his friends as "Henry" or "Hank," was a member of a Chicanx gang from LA's 38th Street who was one of 600 African American and Mexican American individuals

arrested on suspicion of involvement in the murder of José Diaz. The ensu-
ing trial, known as *People v. Zamora* (October 1942–January 1943), was
marked by overt judiciary bias, unlawful use of evidence, and general
miscarriage of justice so blatant that the case was overturned on appeal in
October of 1944 and the prosecutor charged with a violation of the Sixth
Amendment to the US Constitution – but not before Enrique Leyvas and his
cohorts had served hard time in the San Quentin and Folsom prisons.

These are the events dramatized by *Zoot Suit*. The Leyvas character is
Henry Reyna, a pachuco unfairly arrested for murder, and his antagonist
is the quasi-supernatural/quasi-psychological El Pachuco, who guides him,
for better or worse, through his ordeal. El Pachuco is part demon, part angel,
and part ego-ideal, and thanks to its first embodiment by Edward James
Olmos (who played the role in the 1978 premiere, the 1979 Broadway
revival, and the 1981 blockbuster film) has become an icon in American
culture. The importance of this play to the history of American theater has
not always been fully appreciated by journalists and scholars. But the events
surrounding its high-profile 2017 revivals have sparked a new interest in
this vibrant, compelling piece of theater, which retains a vital relevance
nearly forty years after its creation. Consider the opening monologue by El
Pachuco, delivered after he emerges through a slit he has cut in an oversized
newspaper:

> ¿Que le watcha a mis trapos, ese?
> ¿Sabe qué, carnal?
> Estas garras me las planté porque
> Vamos a dejarnos caer un play, sabe?

A mainstream US audience might be forgiven for thinking El Pachuco is
speaking in Spanish, but the language is actually Caló; a highly stylized and
poetic fusion of Hispanized English, anglicized Spanish, the *zincaló* dialect
spoken by Spanish gypsies, and Nahuatl, a language spoken by indigenous
Mesoamericans. The language uses a lot of rhyming, code-switching, and
alterations of phonemes and spellings. It is a uniquely, genuinely American
language and marks its speakers as genuine, if unique, Americans.

With this subversively American language and dress code, *Pachuquismo*
confounds the notion of America as a homogenous society, with a single
language and culture, and exposes that notion as fundamentally racist and
exclusionary. Like the Caló language, the zoot suit is a devout rejection of
the pressure to assimilate with white American culture as a sort of nation-
wide default, but the suit nevertheless embodies the struggle for a modern
Mexican American identity not necessarily tied to elements such as Spanish

Catholicism (and colonialism) or even Native Mesoamerican roots. Instead, as Paz observes, the pachuco lives in search of an identity that insists upon his existence as he is: not North American and not Mexican. Paz describes the pachuco as a reactionary identity that celebrates its differences and welcomes violence toward it as a strange sort of affirmation that fulfills its need to resist. All of this makes the pachuco an ideal signifier for Luis Valdez's dramatization of the story of Henry Reyna.

The longevity of the play is linked directly to this desire to establish an American identity within the so-called American Dream that nevertheless resists a white hegemony. *Zoot Suit* is an ideal case study for illuminating the impact that art, particularly theater, can have on the expression of American multiculturalism. But the producers of the 2017 revival (Valdez' own company El Teatro Campesino, the Center Theatre Group, and the Mark Taper Forum) could hardly have fully reckoned on the events of the 2016 US presidential election on American culture, an election that underscored the need for new affirmative representations of American multiculturalism.

The 2016 US presidential election was dominated by rhetoric that was openly racist, unapologetically divisive, and even gleefully hateful, most of it from the winning candidate, Donald Trump. Trump inaugurated his campaign on June 16, 2015, with these now oft-quoted words:

> When Mexico sends its people, they're not sending their best. They're not sending you. . . . They're sending people that have lots of problems, and they're bringing those problems with them. They're bringing drugs. They're bringing crime. They're rapists. And some, I assume, are good people.

This statement is patently false: there is evidence in fact to the contrary, that immigrants commit crimes at a rate lower than native-born Americans; that while immigration has increased over the past three decades, crime in the United States has decreased; and, furthermore, that immigrants rarely commit the kinds of crimes Trump describes. But in making this claim, Trump was able to capitalize on a long-simmering American xenophobia toward racially diverse immigrants among a percentage of the US electorate that was less interested in fact-checking than it was in giving a face and a name to a diffuse fear that easily conflated Mexicans, Muslims, Africans, and Jews, both immigrants and native-born, into diabolical and collaborative enemies of the state.

The fact that Trump's statements were immediately disproved (and re-disproved each time he reiterated and indeed doubled-down on them) had little impact on the election. In a now well-documented series of events beginning in November of 2016, white supremacists began to openly demonstrate, vandalize, and commit acts of violence against Jews and people of color in Trump's name, particularly in schools and universities. These incidents have been on the rise ever since, with Trump's often explicit endorsement. Trump's election woke Americans up to a new normal in which the conservatism and racism that incited the Zoot Suit Riots seemed unaccountably to have risen from the dead.

The historic popularity of the show, rather than its immediate political relevance, is likely the reason the Center Theatre Group chose to revive *Zoot Suit* in January of 2017. Valdez revised the script in preparation for its 2017 revival at the Mark Taper Forum. This celebrated production starred Demian Bichir in the role of El Pachuco, and the reception was freshly riotous – the show sold out through three extensions in April. Certainly, the production became a site of resistance to the growing power of Trump's racist message. The revision was subtle – minuscule even: a word here, a phrase there, perhaps a quiet indication of a stronger emphasis on this line or that gesture. But the women of the play emerged stronger, with more theatrical impact and depth of character, befitting a society more awake to the perils of male chauvinism. The University of California Santa Cruz presented the second production of this script in May of 2017. This production, directed by Kinan Valdez (son of Luis and co-director of the earlier production at the Taper), was notable for being the first full production sanctioned by El Teatro Campesino and by Luis Valdez to cast a female actor (Gianna DiGregorio Rivera) in the role of El Pachuco in the forty years since the play's inception (Figure 13.1).

This choice was not without some controversy – some parts of which were easier to rationalize than others. First of all, El Pachuco is traditionally cast as male for a variety of reasons, partially because it is seen to be an embodiment of a set of qualities, sometimes called *machismo* or *caballerismo*, that represent a powerful (if chauvinist) ideal of male behavior. Even more significant, perhaps, is the legacy of the iconic character imposed on the role by its first performer, Olmos. For forty years, actors (including Bichir in the 2017 revival) have performed this role more or less as an homage to Olmos's interpretation, mimicking to a greater or lesser degree his gestures and flourishes. But from a dramaturgical perspective, there is nothing in the character of El Pachuco that expressly requires a male portrayal. The zoot suit is, of course, *sine qua non*, but it is well-documented that young Chicana women of the late 70s also sported the zooter style. Furthermore, El Pachuco is not a human being at all, but the avatar of an

Figure 13.1 Zoot Suit, University of California, Santa Cruz
Source: Photography credit Steve DiBartolomeo, 2017

Aztec trickster god of transcendent liminality. Kinan Valdez, in an interview regarding the production, observed that

> my father was actually exploring the mythology of the Aztec deity called Tezcatlipoca, also known as the "Smoking Mirror." Part of what I was interested in was teasing out those mythic elements, and the divine spirit that all mythological creatures have is genderless.[2]

Rivera's performance challenged audiences to enjoy a new appreciation of this dangerous, elegant character and in so doing compelled them to ask questions about their own assumptions regarding sexuality and the qualities attributed to gender.

Luis Valdez stated in a 2014 interview that "the act of bringing people into the theater is the act of creating society, and I think that has to be taken seriously."[3] Since these principles were important to the community of artists and thinkers at UC Santa Cruz, we elected to take such responsibilities as seriously as Luis Valdez had charged and to reflect those values in the work. In this way, we sought to honor *Zoot Suit*'s legacy, which is to remind us that the American Dream, if it does not include all Americans, is no dream at all.

Notes

1 Octavio Paz, The Labyrinth of Solitude: life and thought in Mexico (London: Allan Lane, 1967), p. 5–6.
2 Qtd by Wallace Baine in "UCSC Brings Back the Immortal 'Zoot Suit.'" Santa Cruz Sentinel, 24 May 2017. https://www.santacruzsentinel.com/2017/05/24/ucsc-brings-back-the-immortal-zoot-suit/ 29 Feb 2020.
3 Portillo, Lourdes. Interview with Luis Valdez. PST/LA at the Academy. San Juan Bautista, CA, 7 June, 2014.

14 The Dramaturgical Impulse – or how big is your universe?

Mark Bly

Over a year ago, I was asked to write a contribution to this collection of case studies. The editor shared that the inspiration for the volume had been in part my *Production Notebooks: Theatre in Process*, published in the 1990s, in which eight major dramaturgs in the United States and Canada documented their work through a diary or casebook before and throughout the rehearsal process as they worked on significant productions.[1] Among the projects in the *Notebooks* were ones by Suzan-Lori Parks, Garland Wright, Ntozake Shange, the Franco-American Theatre de la Jeune Lune Company, Robert Wilson, David and Ain Gordon, Jeanine Tesori, Robert Lepage, and Ralph Lemon's astonishing multi-continent dance theater project, *Geography*, on art/race/exile.

The *Notebooks* evolved from and beyond the idea of dramaturgs merely documenting their work and promoting the field of dramaturgy. I discovered during that process that I was increasingly drawn to the actual creative processes that developed between the dramaturgs and their collaborators and their capacity to reveal the layered, often challenging development of each production. Or, as I characterized it in my Introduction to the first volume: "the obstacles encountered, temporary aesthetic detours, and artistic choices made."[2] This "Dramaturgical Impulse" expanded not only my selection of the productions included but what day-to-day questions the dramaturgs might ask about the process while offering fresh perspectives on theatrical practice and on the challenging issues our society faced.

In reading over this new collection of case studies and contemporary responses to race, gender, ethnicity, religion, sexual orientation, disability, incarceration, and geographical considerations, I was thrilled for many reasons, not the least of which was that these studies have continued to explore areas that my production casebooks did but that they have gone beyond them to grapple with even more complex, thorny, urgent, contemporary issues. I found these essays igniting the "Citizen-Dramaturg" in me and awakening thoughts about the "Dramaturgical Impulse" as a quality that profoundly engages our humanness.

In 1940 in Lascaux, France, a complex of caves was discovered, filled with Ice Age paintings made approximately 17,000–20,000 years ago. The walls are filled with astonishing images of bulls, reindeer, aurochs, horses, bison, mammoths, a bird-headed man, and bright, bold, checkerboard shapes that would prefigure Mondrian by more than nineteen millennia. More recent discoveries in South Africa have had momentous implications for the origins of contemporary art-making. In South Africa's Blombos Cave, scientists have found evidence of a Middle Stone Age "art studio" from 75,000–100,000 years ago. Pieces of a silcrete rock were flaked with mysterious crosshatch. Geometric designs on them were found, along with grindstones used to mix red and yellow pigments in abalone shells. Here was early evidence of symbolic thought by modern humans long before the Lascaux Cave paintings, before *Homo sapiens* left Africa for Eurasia. Each time I have read about the latest discoveries on these sites I have wondered: was there an apprentice or observer in those caves who dared to ask a question about these strange, unidentifiable images emerging before them? Did someone dare to ask the artist what were those crosshatch etchings painstakingly scored into the stone in Blombos Cave? In Lascaux Cave, did someone standing next to a Paleolithic Leonardo da Vinci or Frida Kahlo impatiently ask, "Why did you paint a bird-headed man with that bird on a stick and that wounded bison together?" Perhaps there was silence . . . but I'd like to believe that someone asked questions. Someone was curious. Someone wanted to know, integrate, record the story behind those images. Someone had the Dramaturgical Impulse long ago. And it is still in our DNA to ask questions. Asking questions in art-making today it is what we do. What we must do.

Leap back with me to a moment in my own professional evolution – a Yale *Theater* issue that I edited in 1986, in which I interviewed a series of leading dramaturgs across the country, including Arthur Ballet, Oskar Eustis, Anne Cattaneo, and Richard Nelson, about the emerging profession of dramaturgy. The interviews explored a dramaturgical innovation: a "Cambrian Explosion in American Dramaturgy" taking place with the birth of a bastard profession quite distinct from the role of an office-bound literary manager/script reader. Dramaturgy now involved potentially rebellious acts of creation and discovery that could have an ever-evolving role in rehearsal, and in the impact of theater on society. Thirty-three years ago I raised for the first time what was a new notion, the "Questioning Spirit," based on a

Dieter Sturm observation. For me this was a variation on the "Dramaturgical Impulse." It was vital to my process as a dramaturg inside and outside the rehearsal space, as a tool for investigating new work, collaboration, and societal issues.

Over the years since then, wherever I've worked – whether dramaturging a world premiere of *The America Play* or producing *Venus* by playwright Suzan-Lori Parks at the Yale Rep or conducting a workshop at The Kennedy Center or teaching a class for early-career dramaturgs – I have tried to keep in mind for my own awareness two observations, one by the late evolutionary biologist Stephen Jay Gould and the other by Parks herself. From Gould:

> The evolutionary unity of humans with all other organisms is the cardinal message of Darwin's revolution for nature's most arrogant species . . . for each species is unique in its own way; shall we judge among the dance of the bees, the song of the humpback whale, and human intelligence [Figure 14.1]?[3]

And Parks observes, in her early essay "Possession," that "African American history has been unrecorded, dismembered, washed out," and in her

Figure 14.1 The humpback whale speaks for the mysteries of the universes

Source: Getty Images (https://www.gettyimages.com/detail/photo/humpback-swimming-royalty-free-image/123987459?adppopup=true)

stunning contextualization of ideas within the imagery of nature, death, birth, and incubation that follows, we discover:

> The bones tell us what was, is, will be, and because their song is a play – something that through a production actually happens – I'm working theater like an incubator to create "new" historical events. I'm re-remembering and staging historical events which, through their happening on stage, are ripe for inclusion in the canon of history. Theater is an incubator for the creation of historical events-and, as in the case of artificial insemination, the baby is no less human.[4]

The case studies that precede my chapter in *Diversity, Inclusion, and Representation in Contemporary Dramaturgy: Case Studies from the Field* are all unique theatrical and critical demonstrations that represent and challenge the hidden and not-so-hidden prejudices in our theaters, communities, and nation – prejudices that discourage investigations of and resistance to racism, meaningful justice, and equity. In approaching a new play we must, more than ever, have a heightened "social awareness or activism," as the editor has noted. As I write this chapter, physical and ideological walls are erected as emblems of white supremacy in the face of immigrants and citizens; and a degraded Trump presidency feeds an environment of racist outrage and fear. Special-interest EPA appointments have already affected global warming: they have triggered unprecedented offshore drilling for oil and gas, with ship traffic sonar and seismic gun blasts drowning out communication sounds between species of marine life, thus "disturbing feeding, reproduction, and social behavior."[5] Such disturbance in our planet's ecosystems will lead to the worldwide extinction of species, including our own. As if that were not enough, recent judicial appointments have and will affect gender, race, climate change, sexual identification, disability, and ethnic issues, limiting and eroding the civil rights of our citizenry for generations to come. So now it is time for dramaturgs, theater workers, audiences, and all of those who reject limitations and borders to heed the words of one of our first true citizens and revolutionaries, Thomas Paine, who wrote in *The American Crisis*: "But when the country, into which I had just stepped foot, was set on fire about my ears, it was time to stir. It was time for every [hu]man to stir."[6]

One of our most important traits as human beings is curiosity, being interested in others' stories and sharing them: that is, in discovery, not closure. The French-American novelist Anais Nin wrote: "Life shrinks or expands in proportion to one's courage." Her words resonate for me as I write this chapter, with the government's continued push for the alleged "safety" of a border wall; the epic journey by New Horizon's space craft to the Kuiper Belt object, Ultima Thule; and the death, on Christmas Day, 2016, of "the Queen of the Dark," 88-year-old Dr. Vera Rubin. Rubin was credited with nothing less than the discovery of dark matter. Early in the twenty-first century I had, with Artistic Director of the Arena Stage Molly Smith, invited Dr. Rubin to the theater for a new play workshop discussion about Dr. Annie Jump Cannon, a suffragette and major pioneer in American astronomy. Both Dr. Rubin and Dr. Cannon looked where others did not; both had an uncommon curiosity. Dr. Rubin confronted male-dominated obstructionism in the astrophysics community and the Nobel Prize Committee: decade after decade, she stared them down and, indeed, stared beyond them into the heavens as no one had done before.[7]

When I conduct new play workshops or dramaturgy workshops, I inevitably ask the writers or dramaturgs a series of questions informed by the spirits of Dr. Annie Jump Cannon, Dr. Vera Rubin, and the spacecraft *Voyagers 1* and *2*. "How big is your theatrical world? Your theatrical universe?" "Are you open to discovery or do you work best by setting borders?" And "when I go into rehearsal, am I open in my thinking, or do I seek closure in what I have decided that the assembled artists urgently need to know?" If I want to be truly open, I will listen always with the intention that the person speaking has something to teach me, to disrupt my thinking, to open out my horizons. I have shared elsewhere that early in rehearsals I listen to the other collaborators intensely, and I listen to the play until my ears bleed. Then, and only then, will I have something of value to contribute, to share as a Citizen-Artist. How do you listen? Just how curious are you today, inside the rehearsal and outside of it?

Curiosity in human beings matters. When we are not curious we begin to ignore other humans and other creatures of the earth.

Ignoring others' stories leads to a lack of empathy.

Which leads to polarized Us versus Them rhetoric and a thinking that has no interest in those whom we perceive (or ignore) as different from ourselves.

Which can lead to exclusion and often violence – isolationist, colonialist, nationalist, prejudice, discriminatory thinking and behavior, both on an individual and national level.

Our job as artists, students, teachers, and citizens of this country and this world must be to ignite a heightened curiosity and a deeper interest in divergent, inspiring stories and in ancient myths of destruction and renewal that are expressed in words and yet, through their "timeless force," extend and enrich the language of the now, helping us to reinvent form. We must include the past, present, and future and the ever-evolving geological and biological trajectories of this planet and its stories. We must ask the question: who is in control of these stories? How can our theater-making, our pools of profound depth-perception, reflect this? So, how large is your world? How large is your universe? What truly matters now and in the future?

More than forty years ago NASA, led in great part by Dr. Carl Sagan, the astronomer and originator of the iconic television series *Cosmos: A Personal Voyage*, launched *Voyager 1*. It has now left our solar system and is approximately 14 billion miles away from Earth. It has a 12-inch, gold-plated, copper audio-visual disc produced by Sagan, together with Anne Druyan and Timothy Ferris, with "Greetings from the Earth!" It contains messages from fifty-five world languages, a ninety-minute selection of world-wide music, natural sounds ranging from whale sounds to a baby crying, and images from nature showing how varied and beautiful what Sagan calls our "Pale Blue Dot" can be. On February 14, 1990, at Sagan's suggestion, as *Voyager 1* left for the fringes of our solar system, NASA turned the spacecraft around for one last look at Earth and photographed the planet "suspended in a sunbeam."[8] The disc attached to *Voyager 1* is an attempt to reflect the culture and diversity of life on our planet launched as a "shared bottle" into the cosmic ocean: a time capsule that perhaps one day will encounter an advanced spacefaring civilization. No matter what takes place on Earth, this shared bottle looks outward and travels onward. It will be a lonely but wondrous journey of curiosity, leaving behind our anxious reflections. As dramaturgs of the twenty-first century we must push ourselves to bring a spirit of inquiry, challenge, and adventure to our work and to society. How large will our universes be? As large as we can imagine them to be, as Citizen-Artists concerned with the now and its connection to the past and the distant future. We cannot predict with a prophetic lens what will be seen or comprehended beyond where we are at this moment. Will our interstellar neighbors in the distant future, upon opening the "bottle," peer with curiosity into the starry void and discover a Pale Blue Dot? Or will they be puzzled instead by what they see: a lonely Pale Brown Dot?

Notes

1 Mark Bly, *The Production Notebooks: Theater in Process*, vols. I and II (New York: Theater Communications Group, 1996).
2 Ibid., vol. I, ix.

3 Stephen Jay Gould, *The Mismeasurement of Man* (New York: W. W. Norton & Company, 1981).

4 Suzan-Lori Parks, "Possession," in *The America Play and Other Works* (New York: Theatre Communications Group, 1995).

5 Jim Robbins, "Oceans Are Getting Louder, Posing Potential Threats to Marine Life," *Science Times*, *New York Times*, January 22, 2019.

6 Thomas Paine, "Thomas Paine: Collected Writings," available online at www.ushistory.org/paine/crisis/c-07.htm.

7 I highly recommend Losign Ryan Keating, *Losing the Nobel Prize* (New York: W. W. Norton & Company, 2018).

8 Carl Sagan, *Pale Blue Dot: A Vision of the Human Future in Space* (New York: Random House, 1994).

15 Dethroning Ourselves from the Center

Philippa Kelly

Human beings don't change alone – we need other people to help us. This is one of the deep truths of Shakespeare's *King Lear*, as an old man huddles on a blustery heath with his fellow exiles. Shakespeare's Lear has had everything – power, status, the capacity to bequeath vast gifts and thunder his commands – and he unthinkingly gives it all away, assuming an easy exchange of land for vows of love. But the meaning of words can shift from the very instant that they leave one person's mouth and enter the ears of another. Lear learns this, and much more – that his entire identity, for example, is no more stable than a handful of words.

Over the centuries, audiences and critics have speculated a great deal about why Lear's youngest daughter, Cordelia, refuses to give him the terms of love that he desperately wants to hear. A few fawning words in exchange for the best slice of a whole kingdom – it doesn't seem like a lot for her to give. But she has her own reasons for withholding them, and her father finds, to his fury, that he can't make her say them. Cordelia is the first of *Lear*'s rejects, soon joined by the Earl of Kent, Gloucester's son Edgar, and the Fool, all characters who in different ways hold mirrors up to the frail ex-king and his doppelganger, Gloucester. The fact that two once-powerful old men are *willing* to peer, as best they can, into the glasses held up by their companions is the source of their true majesty. It's a majesty that may exist in us all – the capacity not to look away, not to adjust the mirror to a better light: but rather to see ourselves in all our human folly and moral frailty – and to be able to acknowledge the need – and to find the strength – for change.

King Lear is about an old, white, massively entitled patriarch – so why am I contemplating this play in particular as a chapter to conclude a twenty-first-century book about diversity, representation, and inclusion in theater-making? While it's highly irregular for a king ever to give away his crown, this rare ex-king has something in common with any leader, whether of a community group or of a multi-national company. Anyone who knows themselves via their social identity can be stripped of it, "dethroned" from power, shamed, displaced, rejected, rebuffed. Shakespeare's play embodies and scrutinizes loss of belonging, loss of authority, loss of face and, ultimately, *loss itself* as an elemental experience. "To lose," to *feel* the loss, is human.

As we live we try to accumulate – whether it be education, possessions, friends, connections, status, or simply food and a safe place to sleep. And at a certain point – often unknown to us until we have passed it – we begin the first of what may be one or many reversals of fortune. What we have accumulated is suddenly depleted or gone, and we may even feel invisible.

Lear's great reversal doesn't come till very late, when he knows that death is knocking at the door. This knock is what prompts his initial court scene, his sudden and shocking break from protocol: because he knows inside himself that courtly protocol and regal furs and gowns cannot quiet that insistent knock of death or make it go to another door. Hence his sudden command for love: his wish to spend his last days in Cordelia's "kind nursery," and, when she is gone, his attempt to insulate himself from loneliness with a hundred knights (even fifty, even twenty-five). How aptly does he express the reek of frail, lonely humanness: "Let me wipe it first," he says of his hand. It is no longer the hand that those beneath him were once privileged to kiss. It is simply a hand, "smell[ing] of mortality." Loneliness is terrifying, and this ex-regent, ex-CEO, ex-Big Guy, is learning the alien truth of his own mere humanness. We are all kings until we are told that we are not, and we are all of us beggars-in-waiting. Lear learns to see true majesty in every human being, and that to be a simple human among humans is not a source of shame but a thing of great dignity.

"Patience! Patience I need!" cries the old man. The strength to endure while we absorb the need to change and make the change itself – this is what Lear comes to require of himself: "Let me not be mad, not mad, sweet heaven." And in reflecting on equity, diversity, representation, and inclusion in concert with this play, I see not just the theme of change, but that of surrender. Surrender doesn't have to be "giving in" – it can also reflect the capacity to slough off what we've had, who we've assumed we were. Through surrender we may find that we are okay without formerly cherished plumes and titles, gold or palatial homes, or even affirmations of our unique value. There is a different kind of wealth in new perception. As human beings (*not* locked, it turns out, in identities that we may have groomed for decades) we can, and even must, differently occupy places, self-images, roles in conversations. Nothing about us is immortal, least of all our self-images and opinions.